MEDIA: FROM CHAOS TO CLARITY

FIVE GLOBAL TRUTHS THAT MAKE SENSE OF A MESSY MEDIA WORLD
(Second Edition)

D1246628

By Judy Ungar Franks

MEDIA: FROM CHAOS TO CLARITY

FIVE GLOBAL TRUTHS THAT MAKE SENSE OF A MESSY MEDIA WORLD (Second Edition)

By Judy Ungar Franks

The Marketing Democracy, Ltd.
2018, USA, Chicago

Media: From Chaos to Clarity
Five Global Truths That Make Sense of a Messy Media
World By Judy Ungar Franks
Second Edition Copyright © 2018 by The Marketing Democracy, Ltd.

ISBN: 978-0-9834662-3-9

Printed in the United States of America by CreateSpace (a division of Amazon)
10 9 8 7 6 5 4 3 2 1

^{the}marketing Democracy   The Marketing Democracy, Ltd.

Web site: www.themarketingdemocracy.com

For James

Thank you for showing me that you can find clarity in chaos if you are willing look at the world in entirely new ways.

TABLE OF CONTENTS

FOREWORD

A ROLLERCOASTER RIDE THROUGH MEDIA

The first edition of Judy Franks's text, *Media: From Chaos to Clarity*, was published in 2011. I was privileged to write the foreword for that book, which put forth a revolutionary view of the evolving media landscape and the impact of such profound changes on the media and marketing industries. Here, we meet again. And times continue to change. These industries look radically different today than they did just a few short years ago when the first edition was published.

Traditionally, most second editions hew to much the same framework as the first. The author makes a few content changes, updates a few charts, throws in a new quip or two and is done with the task. New publication date, new cover, and, voilà—a 2nd Edition. That's not the case with Judy's media book.

Instead, the entire premise of the first edition had to be challenged: did those Five Global Truths that Judy introduced in the first edition hold up to all the chaos that exists in the media landscape today? Or did they need to be scrapped? They're tough questions, but because the field has changed so radically over the past seven years, they had to be asked.

For those of you who have any experience in the media and/or marketing industries, you'll find the views and comments in this text both interesting and challenging. You'll see how the industry forged ahead with what it thought it knew to be true, applying old thinking and old rules to a new media world. Many of you are in the throes of an unprecedented technology transformation that is reshaping your careers. But when you take a peek under the hood, you'll soon discover that this new technology isn't as innovative as it seems. Instead, we're using it to automate old thinking.

For many, this book will be like a rollercoaster ride with high and low points and many in-betweens in terms of concepts, methodologies, approaches and applications. This is a highly creative perspective on what is often considered a highly formulaic discipline. Judy's book offers Big Thinking and Big Ideas.

Because the field has changed, you'll need a guide. Judy provides that leadership beautifully. She describes, compares, and illustrates the industry's shifts in a way any reader can understand. She defines and explains new terms, concepts, and ideas—many of which are not normally found in a media text. But despite these new terms and changes to the field, you'll find that the framework Judy offered in the first edition still holds true today. Her Five Global Media Truths—Convergence, Symbiosis, Circuits, Brands and Economics—make eminently good sense for understanding media behavior: both at the dawn of the digital media era, and certainly today.

Make no mistake, this is not a traditional "how to" media text, suitable for mid-to-junior level employees. Instead, it is a managerial view of the entire spectrum of message distribution in a digital media world which has seemingly unlimited potential and possibilities. You'll find no "best practices" or "step-by-step processes." That is because, as Judy so eloquently argues, every media experience is essentially unique.

Judy shares a new energy formula that places channels at the very end and, frankly, in the lowest priority order. Great content is the fuel that can provoke real consumers—not faceless populations—but rather individuals who have heads and hearts. In Judy's view, channels are nothing more than tools that consumers use to shape and share this content with others in their networks. It is around, through, and within these personally developed networks and circuits that true value is generated. Ultimately, Judy argues, it is the value created that is important, not just the number of eyes or ears exposed to the message.

This 2nd Edition of *Media: From Chaos to Clarity* is unlike any media discussion you have ever seen before. That is, unless you read the first edition. Many readers will be challenged by the approach taken in this book. And, most likely, those who have some experience in the field will be the most challenged. That's because what you thought you knew, what you have been told, and what you were planning to do with all that emerging marketing automation and Big Data will have to be reconsidered for this new world of Global Truths. You will have to re-tool for a new paradigm in which your creativity and thoughtfulness will be more valuable than your ability to count impressions, clicks, and views. Your years of experience in the field might only offer you the stamina and the courage to try a new approach. For beginners who have not been tainted by existing practices, that's great news. For others, not so much.

So, my advice to you is to read on. Compare what you find in the pages that follow with your own experience in today's rapidly evolving and emerging marketplace. If you open your mind, you may see how closely your personal experiences in human communication mirror the media world that Judy envisions in this text. In short, media today is what you make of it. It's up to you, and that can be a most illuminating and energizing way to consider your future.

Don Schultz
Professor, Emeritus-in-Service
Northwestern University, Medill School

PREFACE

Before we spend some quality time together, I owe you an introduction. An author should not just show up uninvited. You may have picked up this book because you work in media or are interested in the field. Perhaps you heard the text was "a good read" that offers insight into the media world today. Maybe the book was assigned to you as required reading, and you really had no choice! Regardless of your reason for opening this book, you need to be assured that your time will be well spent, and that you'll leave with a better understanding of the messy media world that surrounds us.

My name is Judy Ungar Franks, and I am a full-time clinical faculty member at Northwestern University's Medill School of Journalism, Media and Integrated Marketing Communications. I teach both media and consumer insight courses in Medill's undergraduate and graduate IMC programs. Since joining the faculty in the fall of 2008, I have been named to the Northwestern University Associated Student Government Faculty Honor Roll four times, and in 2016, I was named IMC Teacher of the Year by the MSIMC graduating class.

When I am not in the classroom, I help to design executive education programming for Medill IMC alumni and I also collaborate with other faculty members on research related to media economics and technology. Some of you may know me as a visiting faculty member of the Coursera/Northwestern MOOC on Social Media Marketing.

Prior to joining the faculty of Northwestern University, I spent 23 years working in the advertising and media services agency world. I rose to the executive leadership ranks of

Chicago's leading advertising and media services agencies: Leo Burnett, Euro RSCG Chicago (formerly known as TLK), Starcom and Energy BBDO.

During my tenure in the agency world, media changed exponentially. I experienced these changes firsthand via a myriad of client situations, customer targets and global markets. In every case, the media plans we designed and recommended to our clients radically changed from an emphasis on television (with a smattering of other media for good measure), to a sophisticated combination of video, audio, text and social messages that traversed every screen imaginable.

We cobbled together media strategies and plans without a reliable compass. We relied on established theories of media effects that were left over from a pre-digital media world, and then augmented those theories with data from market-mix models and real-time customer behavior. In essence, we created coping mechanisms for navigating uncharted waters.

When I left the agency world to join Northwestern's faculty back in 2008, my first order of business was to develop a new media course for the IMC program. When I set out to find a contemporary text for the course, I couldn't find one that described the media mess that we were dealing with in the real world. Many textbooks still described media as it was over 25 years ago. They falsely assumed that the thinking and models that applied to a non-digital media world still made sense. Sure, they covered "new" and "emerging" outlets such as digital, social and mobile media. But they did so as if these media were simply additional choices to consider when building a media plan. They didn't address the paradigm shift that marketers, media planners and the media were actually dealing with.

I soon discovered that the problem extended beyond old, dusty textbooks. Through work at my consulting firm, The Marketing Democracy, I realized that marketers were still trying to navigate these new waters with a broken compass. The media world had changed, yet marketers were still using an approach to media planning and implementation from a long-gone era.

In 2011, I published the first edition of *Media: From Chaos to Clarity* to offer an explanation for what was transpiring in the media world. The book introduced "Five Global Truths" that made sense of a messy media world. Each of the Truths offered a plausible explanation for unprecedented changes in the media that, on the surface, looked like a bunch of chaos. *Media: From Chaos to Clarity* also offered a new interpretation of how media worked together to create truly exponential outcomes.

When I first published *Media: From Chaos to Clarity*, the Five Global Truths were emerging concepts. I didn't know with certainty whether a compass with five navigational vectors (a.k.a Truths) would lead us in the right direction. More time needed to pass, and more media chaos needed to unfold before we could know whether the "Five Global Truths"—both individually and collectively—would remain a sound framework for understanding the continued evolution of the media.

In late 2017, I began to revisit these ideas. Time didn't stand still and the media and marketing world certainly didn't either! The media continued to evolve in messy ways—far beyond what was in our line of sight back in 2011. Meanwhile, advances in technology profoundly impacted how marketers approached media planning and buying. Marketers began to automate several marketing functions by leveraging the power of algorithms and Big Data. Would the Five Global Truths hold up in this current landscape?

In this edition, we will find that the Five Global Truths are even more relevant today than they were when *Media: From Chaos to Clarity* was first published. We will also take a look at how the industry is coping with all this change. Traveling through chaos isn't easy. But, with the Five Global Truths as a compass, we can navigate the existing media landscape and envision a road map for where we are headed with more clarity.

I look forward to sharing my interpretation with you in the coming chapters of the book. You may not agree with every point. Nor will every recommendation be relevant to you. But I hope you will be inspired to look at the messy media world in a whole new light. And I hope that the Five Global Truths will, in some way, help you to thrive in your pursuits.

Best Wishes,

Judy Ungar Franks

CHAPTER ONE

ONCE UPON A TIME

Once upon a time and not too long ago, the media, for all its variety, was fairly predictable. Newspapers delivered the daily news on our doorsteps. Magazines fueled our passions. Television was "must-see." Radio dominated drive time. And computers put a world of information at our fingertips. With reasonable accuracy, we could understand media audiences and predict the return on investments when we used various media to connect these audiences with brands.

Welcome to Media Chaos

Now, virtually all of those dependable, measurable media models are undergoing revolutionary change. Welcome to media chaos. We are living in what may be the most exciting and transformative time in the history of the media, and it's messy. What was once an orderly media system with predictable audiences and dependable business models has turned into a cross-channel firestorm that is exploding and imploding all at once. It's chaos! Literally.

Unfortunately, human beings aren't hardwired to deal with chaos. We like to know what to expect. We crave a sense of order. But, despite our desire for order, we deal with chaos in all aspects of our lives every day. When we walk out the door we enter a chaotic world, and we don't give it much thought.

Perhaps we have developed coping mechanisms, a series of rituals that create some sense of order and purpose in our world despite the mess that surrounds us. These beliefs, or Truths, enable us to navigate through and even thrive in chaos.

We Need to Navigate Our Way Through Media Chaos

That's what this book is about. It's about new ways to talk and think about the media world in chaos. We need to face the media world's unprecedented transformation—and teach ourselves and others what's actually going on. Not what used to happen in a more orderly media world, but what is happening now. If we intend to thrive during this period of extreme uncertainty and transformational change, we'll need to find truths that can help us to navigate the chaos.

It's a top-to-bottom job. And bottom to top. Students still need to learn how to become effective marketers, marketers still need to build brands and drive commerce, and media companies still need to distribute great content and make a profit while they're at it. And we all need to figure out how to talk to each other.

Unfortunately, moving forward is easier said than done because we're still working with old systems that don't account for the new reality of the media. As a result, many conversations happening (in the boardroom *and* the classroom) are far from productive.

Let's Drop the Unhelpful Theories

First, we need to strike a few theories from our collective consciousness in order to move forward. Remember: Nothing good ever comes from doom and gloom, the past is not always a window to the future, and technology, for all its glitz and glory, isn't the full story.

The Apocalypse Theory
(or the Sky Is Falling)

It's time to set the record straight. It isn't all doom and gloom, despite what the naysayers are saying (and, by the way, they make money by creating drama). Nothing is dying that doesn't deserve to die off on its own. We are confusing the death of old business models with the death of traditional media themselves. If you've been making money from business models that have fallen apart and you're not prepared to change, maybe you are in trouble. But the notion that new media is killing old media is simply untrue. Nothing dies unless it's weak to begin with. If a weak organism catches a virus, it dies. If a healthy organism catches a virus, it fights it off and actually becomes stronger.

What Is Past Is Prologue Theory
(or Apply Old Methods to New Media)

We can never truly move forward without an understanding of our past. But understanding the past and remaining stuck in the past are two very different things. The old rules of media that were based upon fixed distribution channels, predictive audience aggregation and response functions simply cannot cope with the dynamics and complexity of the chaos. In fact, we are experiencing our version of quantum media that requires quantum media thinking. The old, Newtonian rules simply do not apply.

Carpe Technology Diem
(or Technology Rules Everything)

Every day, a new technology springs up that becomes the darling of the industry and the focus of our attention. But these are usually just distractions. Technology is transient! Wait 10 minutes and it will change. The fleeting nature of technology is no surprise: Moore's Law mandates it. If we build marketing practices around technology, we need to be prepared for those practices to have a short shelf life.

We Can Find Truths in the Chaos Itself

Moving forward, perhaps the best place to find answers is in the chaos itself. That's where the Five Global Truths that make sense out of a messy media world emerged from.

We didn't simply "land" on these truths. Each one only became apparent after we investigated the new function of the media themselves. Some new technology had to emerge, changing what was possible. And some pioneer had to recognize the potential of this technology. The journey certainly isn't easy. But if we keep our line of sight on what is truly possible, we can realize a new truth.

These phases in the narrative of the Five Global Truths serve as an outline for the story that will unfold in the following pages:

The Technology: Something structurally changed.
The Pioneer: Someone had an "aha" moment.
The Journey: Sometimes we stumble along the way.
The Truth: Somehow, it all makes sense.

If we can navigate using the Five Global Truths, we will be poised to flourish in media chaos and actually learn to enjoy it!

CHAPTER TWO

THE JOURNEY THROUGH MEDIA TIME

Just one short generation ago, we lived and marketed in the Newtonian Media Era. The media systems were relatively stable, and the laws of marketing were absolute. Think about it. Our choices were limited to four major "above the line" media: television, radio, print and out of home. Each medium drew mass audiences in relatively predictable patterns, and we knew how to develop strategies both within and across media to reach audiences and accumulate advertising effects. Even the most coveted medium of all, word of mouth, was simply a matter of engaging in and inspiring a one-on-one conversation.

The Newtonian Media Era Was Predictable

In the Newtonian Media Era, we planned media allocations with authority and we predicted outcomes based upon what were, at the time, irrefutable laws of media dynamics.

- *The Law of Recency (Erwin Ephron):*
  Advertising continuity and weekly reach are the best media scheduling practices to intercept a shopper as close to the purchase occasion as possible.

- *The Law of AdStock (Simon Broadbent):*
  Advertising accumulates effects over time (i.e., builds AdStock) and up to a point when it will begin to decay (half-life) without further support.
- *The Law of Effective Reach (Herb Krugman):*
  Consumers are more likely to respond after three exposures to a commercial message.

Although the laws conflicted with each other, it didn't matter. Marketers could subscribe to a particular theory of how advertising worked, and media planners could build a media plan that would emulate the theory in the real world. Things didn't change all that much from the plan "on paper" to the plan "in market." We were able to model results with relative statistical certainty.

Chaos Begins to Emerge

During the late 20th century, things began to change. We began to see a breakdown in the certainty of both legacy systems (the media themselves) and legacy thinking (those irrefutable laws). The world became less predictable, and so did our outcomes in the marketplace. The early signs of chaos began to emerge. Let's call this period the Era of Media Relativity.

Why was the media world becoming less certain? Actually, the biggest media transformation of modern times, digital media, was not yet part of the story. While digital marketing did emerge toward the end of the 20th century, it really didn't play much of a role in the transformation taking place during the Era of Media Relativity. Rather, the true transformation was caused by the legacy media themselves.

During the late 20th century, media capacity expanded beyond our wildest imaginations. The legacy media went through a radical transformation as the number of options across every channel—TV, magazines, radio, etc.—expanded. And the transformation was not a straight-line trajectory of what we already knew and accepted as true. The changes we were seeing in the media were paradoxical and downright challenging to the conventions of our Newtonian media minds.

Media Becomes Both Mass and Niche

As capacity expanded and more options became available, media began to take on properties of both mass and niche at the same time. For example, television could now attract mass audiences to primetime "event" shows, while also catering to the niche tastes of gardeners, cooks or fishermen through specialty cable networks. Magazines in the general interest and women's service categories still enjoyed mass circulation figures while special interest publications could also thrive by selling just a few hundred thousand copies. AM news/talk radio stations could still reach the majority of the local market during drive time while a jazz station could cater to the tastes of a select audience on the FM band. And so on.

According to Newtonian media thinking, mass and niche should be diametrically opposed. In the classical calculations of reach and frequency, these two factors are mathematical tradeoffs. How could media take on both properties at once? This paradox simply didn't fit the commonly accepted understanding of how the media work.

Media Audiences Become Less Predictable

The rapid expansion of media choices also made it increasingly difficult to predict audience exposure with absolute certainty. Audiences became much more dynamic and difficult to pin down both within and across media. While, historically, we could count audience exposures with a fair degree of certainty, we now had to settle for probabilities and "opportunities to see" (OTS).

To make matters worse, that emerging medium called "digital" had a completely different set of audience measurement rules associated with search and direct response that made no sense in a world that was dominated by the laws of reach and frequency. Ironically, the new digital media could be measured in more absolute terms while the established legacy media became more relative in their performance.

The Media World Changes but Media Laws Stay the Same

Would the Era of Media Relativity create a new operating system and displace all of our Newtonian media laws? We needed our version of Heisenberg's Uncertainty Principle and the idea that "it all depends upon your point of view."

Perhaps the birth of Context Planning (also known as Connection Planning or Communication Planning) was our answer to the relative state of the media. Now, in addition to counting, we looked for context and congruence. Could we expect the brand to show up in this particular context? Would the media placement fit? This method made media selection more open for interpretation and judgment from the marketer, the account planner, the media planner and the consumer.

Unfortunately, all the scholarship both in academia and in industry could not definitively support whether media congruence improves advertising effects. As a result, Context Planning did not displace those old, Newtonian rules. Instead, the industry continued to apply these rules to a media world that simply didn't behave the way it used to.

Media Continues to Change Exponentially

Thank goodness, it really doesn't matter anymore. The Era of Media Relativity is over. Welcome to the Era of Exponential Effects. The media landscape is changing around us in real time and in such profound ways that the situation can only be described as exponential. Everything we knew to be true is now in question. The media seem to be propelled by completely new laws of energy that have exponential effects on marketing outcomes.

The Three Cs Fuel This New Era

The Era of Exponential Effects is fueled by the three Cs: content, consumers and channels. There is nothing new about the three primary ingredients in this equation. What has changed profoundly is the relationship of the three Cs to each other and the unfathomable outcomes when they work well together.

1.   *Content* is no longer the stuff that fills stable media systems; rather, it is the magnet that attracts audiences and involves them in the marketing process.
2.   *Consumers* have evolved from recipients of marketing to accelerants of marketing. They are the most powerful channel in the entire media system.
3.   *Channels* are now the ultimate wild card in the marketing plan. Channels are no longer controlled distribution systems for marketing messages, but rather the mechanism by which consumers can see, shape, share or reject marketing messages. Welcome to chaos!

C (1): Content

The roles played by content and channels are often confused. So let's set the record straight. Media cannot attract audiences: only content has the power to attract and engage an audience. Content is the glue that holds everything together. Without *great* content, channels lose their importance. The channels themselves no longer have the capability to attract and sustain an audience. They are nothing more than transient pipeline.

Content is the Audience Magnet

Once upon a time, the individual channels could build audiences on their own. Not anymore. The ability of any single channel to create an audience dissipated as soon as consumers were faced with an abundance of choice. Once the media began to expand beyond a few limited options, consumers had the choice to opt in to specific content offerings that suited their interests. The content distributed by a particular channel became the audience magnet rather than the channel itself.

Dr. Mark Maiville presented this finding to the ARF Audience Measurement Symposium back in 2007. His work, "A Thin Sliced World: New Methods, Models and Systems for Media Audience Analysis," demonstrated that media audiences are nothing more than millions of individual consumers exercising their content preferences on available channels. Consumers find content that is relevant to them, and they ignore the rest.

Dr. Mark Maiville was not alone. Others supported the idea that media audiences are attracted to content, and not to the channel itself. Professor Philip Napoli in his seminal work *Audience Economics* describes a *dual product marketplace* whereby media produce a *content product* in order to attract an *audience product* that media companies can then monetize through the sale of audience impressions to advertisers. Napoli's explanation of Media Economics focuses on the quality of the content product as a means of attracting audiences that advertisers then wish to engage with.

Only Truly Great Content Stands a Chance

In this new Era of Exponential Effects, media companies are not the only ones who must shift their focus to the production and distribution of *great* content in order to engage with audiences. Marketers must take note as well. No longer will mediocre marketing content be good enough. Only content that is truly *great* regardless of who produces it stands a chance in this new media world.

Great content can traverse the boundaries of any particular media channel to become what we now call a transmedia experience. In his 2006 book, *Convergence Culture*, Henry Jenkins describes a world where content creators can tell stories across media channels and "in ways that each medium makes distinctive contributions to our collective understanding." An engaged fan is more than willing to traverse channels to deepen his or her experience with a transmedia story.

While the entertainment industry is quickly adopting a transmedia content model, the marketing industry has been slow to follow. Marketers still craft individual channel strategies and then develop content to suit the channel. Transmedia marketing campaigns are still few and far between. In this new era, marketers must shift their focus toward the creation of compelling content that is suited for a transmedia experience.

C(2): Consumers

In the Era of Exponential Effects, consumers are no longer recipients; they are now accelerants. They used to be the end point; now they are a powerful intermediary. Today's consumers can amplify marketing messages by exponential measures—by the size of their networks and at the speed of their connections.

"Reach" Takes on a Whole New Meaning

This phenomenon creates a new reach potential beyond anyone's wildest dreams. How many consumers can we reach in the Era of Exponential Effects? The answer: We truly don't know. Reach takes on a whole new meaning. We can only measure the first step in a multi-step process where consumers quickly take over and control the ultimate reach of our efforts.

Reach still begins as a measure of the opportunity to see a brand's message that was placed in a particular medium. That used to be the end point of the calculation, but now it's just the first step of a potentially exponential experience. A portion of the audiences will actually see/hear/experience the message, and a portion of them will become truly engaged. An engaged consumer now has the ability to perpetuate and accelerate a brand's message among his or her personal networks and across a myriad of media channels.

Each individual network offers a whole new audience to the marketing message—one that was not planned for or controlled by the marketer (or the media for that matter). The consumer now acts as a media channel with its own built-in audience (friends, fans, followers, email lists etc.). And the cycle continues.

So what is the true reach of a media plan? It depends on two key factors: How many people did you engage in the first place? And how far and wide did the message travel among each engaged consumer's network? The answer to both questions is: "We really don't know!"

Consumers Can Accelerate a Message's Demise, Too

There is also a downside to this consumer dynamic: consumers now have the ability to accelerate the demise of ineffective marketing communication. Consumers always had the power to avoid and ignore commercial messages in any channel. Now it's just more transparent to the marketer.

But consumer avoidance isn't the full story. For instance, imagine if you anger somebody. What happens when consumers can register their disdain across social media channels that have exponential reach potential? You are left with contra-marketing initiatives that can overpower the brand's own voice.

C (3): Channels

Channels have become the real wild card in the equation. What was once a relatively fixed distribution system for content has now become incredibly amorphous and downright chaotic. What happened? Welcome to the digital media revolution.

The Digital Revolution Upends Channels

In the first decade of the 21st century, digital was no longer something tied to a computer screen; rather, nearly every media platform known to man became digital in some form. This digital transformation destabilized the entire media ecosystem in two fundamental ways. First, legacy media companies no longer had a proprietary hold on distribution. For next to no cost, anyone could enter the media business by launching a digital media channel.

Second, the digitized nature of the media enabled consumers to displace content from one channel and send it along another digital pathway without much, if any, intervention from the content producer. Content could fall right through the cracks or travel beyond our wildest imaginations.

In This New Era, What's the Role of a Media Plan?

This shift raises a few questions: If media channels are no longer fixed distribution systems that are managed solely by media companies and if content can easily jump from one channel to another, what is the value of a media plan? Are marketers clinging to the notion that they still have control over the brand experience? Has the media plan become nothing more than an expensive piece of paper that yields a false sense of security?

Any approach that focuses on channels loses sight of the potential of this new media era that prioritizes content and its consumer-powered acceleration. That doesn't mean we should walk away from a blueprint, but we do have to acknowledge two fundamental changes to the contemporary media plan. First, the pathways are now determined by both the professional and the consumer. Second, these pathways cannot be fully charted until the journey is complete.

Thank goodness consumers are now co-creators in this process. They are having a much easier time than both marketers and media companies living in media chaos. They don't ask why; they simply consume unfathomable amounts of all types of media and shape their experiences as they go. We in the industry—along with those who study it—are stuck with the why.

Integrated Marketing Communications (IMC) cannot deteriorate into chaos simply because we aren't equipped to wrap our heads around the exponential changes in the media universe. It's time to make sense of the messy media world. It's time to uncover the Global Truths.

CHAPTER THREE

THE FIVE GLOBAL TRUTHS

How can we harness the power and potential of C^3—content, consumers and channels? It's easier said than done! When one of the three key elements—channels—is in a state of total flux, and the other two are exhibiting their own dynamics, we're looking at a challenge of some size.

Perhaps if we look beyond all the disruptions and distractions, we might be able to see patterns and purpose. Maybe media chaos isn't so complex after all. Einstein said it best: "If you can't explain it simply, you don't understand it well enough." Is it possible that there are simple explanations for the seismic shifts in the media universe?

There are Simple Explanations Beneath the Chaos

Oftentimes, there are simple explanations buried beneath all the problems. You simply have to get to the root of the problem! As a first step, let's lay the problems out on the table. When you listen to all the complaints that run rampant in the press, in the conference rooms of Fortune 500 companies and their marketing services agencies and among the media themselves, you can begin to classify the issues into five macro themes.

Each of the five problems listed here reveals an underlying explanation: a core truth that helps us understand this new media world we're living in. Quite often, these problems offer paths to new opportunities. And they definitely lead to new ways of looking at the world of media.

Problem #1: Media Identity Crisis

As we mentioned earlier, media channels used to be separate and distinct from one another. Each had a specific function/utility in our lives. We used to talk on phones, watch video content on televisions and surf for information on computers.

Now? The media are tripping over each other! We can do practically all of the above on any screen device. How can we tell the media apart? How do we know when to use specific media and for what purpose? What content belongs on what channel?

Underlying Explanation: Convergence

Let's take another look at the media identity crisis. Perhaps the orientation of the media has shifted. What used to be separate and distinct has merged. The media can now be explained with one word: convergence. Media are becoming strikingly similar.

And most of them are interconnecting and converging through some sort of digital interface. Each new delivery mechanism serves to blur the lines further. What was once separate is now the same. And, more often than not, it comes with a screen!

Problem #2: Winners and Losers

There is so much "new media" to contend with every day, how can we predict the winners and the losers? When deciding how to manage a media budget, this is no small question. Which media deserves our attention and investment of time and resources? Which media should bear the inevitable budget cut? Which media will be around in the next five years, three years or even one year?

These are some of the questions that we need to keep asking—particularly since the media landscape keeps on changing. We want to invest in the winners and not spend our budgets on the losers. That's true for venture capitalists, marketers and media professionals themselves.

Underlying Explanation: Symbiosis

Perhaps there are no clear winners or losers anymore. Instead, emerging media tend align themselves with existing media to create mutually beneficial relationships. The age-old notion of survival of the fittest is giving way to a more cooperative and collaborative system: symbiosis. The media do not kill each other; instead they can actually reinforce each other! Just watch any consumer engage with media and you will quickly discover that they are willing to cross channels and use multiple devices to more deeply engage with content that touches their head and/or their heart.

It took a while, but media companies are catching on by creating cross-platform destinations to engage with audiences. Now marketers need to follow suit and celebrate the true potential of integrated marketing communications: the integration of engaging consumer experiences that are strengthened by channels working together.

Disappointed? There's more drama in "winners and losers," but the fact remains: media collaborate despite our best efforts to pit them against each other. While it's true that individual media brands may come and go, that's "creative destruction" at work. Don't confuse evolution with extinction.

Problem #3: Faulty Wiring

Content doesn't stay put anymore. Instead, it goes

wherever consumers want it to go. We can try to control it, but it seems to leak, short-circuit and show up on different pathways. Not only that, but content rarely travels untouched across a distribution pathway without something happening to it. Content either vaporizes or it lands on alternate distribution pathways or it attracts additional comment—for better or worse. That being the case, how can we build marketing plans with any confidence that the content we place on any particular channel will travel from Point A to Point B with limited disruption? Previously, this was never a problem. Now it is.

Underlying Explanation: Circuits

Perhaps the media aren't faulty at all. It's just that programmers and marketers are no longer in control of media circuits; consumers are. Some call this phenomenon "pull marketing." But what we are seeing is far more profound than pull. Rather, consumers can displace content from any media channel and either: (1) vaporize it because it isn't any good or (2) share great content across other channels.

We used to believe that each medium functioned as a closed circuit that ran in parallel to other media. Thanks to convergence, the circuits are now open and content can flow freely across channels. This has thrown our ability to accurately measure the reach and frequency of our marketing efforts right out the window. Consumers can accelerate content along open media circuits at what we will refer to as "the speed of share." And the impact of this type of content acceleration along open circuits is truly exponential.

Problem #4: Living Beyond Purpose

Have the media outlived their respective functions? Once upon a time, media distribution technology was relatively limited and quite expensive. We needed towers to broadcast signals to a designated market area (DMA). We needed elaborate distribution networks to access content on the printed page. Our choices were bound by the bandwidth of the spectrum and the cost of paper, ink and postage. Specific media used to be necessary distribution pathways to reach specific audiences. To some extent, they had audience exclusivity.

Today, thanks to digital technology, it seems that no single medium has an "exclusive" on either its method of distribution or the audience it serves. The media have become functionally redundant. Those old distribution silos that insulated media from competition have fallen by the wayside. Consumers have more choices than ever before. Media have more competitors than ever before. When no single media company can claim exclusive ownership of its distribution pathway or the audience it serves, what's left for them? How can media remain important in the hearts and minds of their audiences?

Underling Explanation: Brands

While it may be true that many media have outlived their functional utility, perhaps media can take on new purpose if we reframe them not as products but as brands. Brands are as strong as the promises they keep. And, for media companies, the content they produce and distribute is an ongoing testament to that promise. Only when their content fulfills the wants and needs of audiences better than anyone else's can media gain a lasting place in the hearts and minds of audiences.

The relationship between audience and content can transcend the boundaries of any channel and enable a media brand to remain relevant today, tomorrow and well into the future. This is what we mean by a "transmedia" brand: a media brand that stands for a promise that is bigger than any particular channel that delivers the promise.

For transmedia brands, channels become flexible tools that deliver the best content experience imaginable given the current state of the media landscape—whatever that may be. When a channel no longer serves its functional purpose, a transmedia brand can adapt and deliver its content promise in new ways without collapsing under the weight of a failing distribution strategy.

Media brands are faced with all kinds of competition for the time and attention of audiences. They now compete with other media brands that historically weren't a threat. Thanks to the force of convergence, the silos that used to confine media to specific distribution channels are long gone: media no longer need to stay in their own lane. Even those marketers who used to subsidize media companies with advertising revenue are becoming new forms of competition. Many marketers have their own distribution networks to deliver engaging, high quality content experiences directly to their customer base.

In a new media world that favors brands, marketers have a distinct advantage. They already understand branding practices. The media piece is relatively easy in comparison. Media companies will have to catch up quickly if they want to survive and thrive among all the competition they face today.

Problem #5: Who Pays the Bills?

Does anyone know how to make money anymore? Nothing is sustainable when it's heavily discounted or given away for free. Yet, in the early days of digital media, that's exactly what we did. We often gave access to content away for free, either because we thought it didn't matter or because we assumed that no one would pay for it. Plus, any digital advertising that wasn't offered as "added value" onto a legacy media buy was also deeply discounted. We trained a generation of marketers to pay only pennies on the dollar for access to audiences in digital media.

As a result, we have a generation of audiences who expect either free or very low-cost access to content and we have a generation of marketers who are only willing to pay extremely low rates when an audience clicks on their ads. Since so much of the media economy has shifted over to digital media, this is causing a major disruption to business models across the entire media ecosystem.

Meanwhile, great content is still very expensive to produce. Here's the reality: someone has to pay for it. Either consumers will have to pay, or marketers will have to step up. But the last thing marketers want to do is pay more for advertising. They are looking to contain and even reduce their expenses. Some are trying to bypass paid media altogether. If no one is willing to pay their fair share, what's the new financial formula for success?

Underlying Explanation: Economics

Media economics still operates by the laws of supply and demand. However, in the media landscape we are experiencing today, the supply and demand curves are literally flipped. Once upon a time, the media themselves were in limited supply. Now, we have more media than we know what to do with. And consumers are less inclined to pay for distribution that is transient or redundant. Consumers are more than willing to abandon legacy distributors in favor of more cost-effective alternatives.

Meanwhile, the supply of high quality content isn't expanding at the same rate. As a result, media companies are in heated competition to win the bidding wars for great content. And as we already learned, without great content, media channels are nothing more than empty pipes.

Content economics is also the driving force behind two very different advertising marketplaces we are seeing today.

Those media companies who have a lock on high quality content can create private marketplaces and still command premium prices for their limited and highly valued advertising inventory. Everyone else is facing new forms of competition for their fair share of advertising revenue as the overall supply of ad-supported content has swelled.

All this excess content has created the fuel for a new advertising marketplace: open exchanges. These exchanges allow advertisers to bid on audiences at the lowest possible price. Without great content, media companies are forced to compete for advertising revenue through a transactional model that behaves like a commodities exchange. It's a slippery slope and there's only one way to avoid it: great content.

Economics is the final challenge. We need to arrive at a business model that delivers value to marketers and allows media management to make an honest profit. Media profits fuel investments in content. And high quality content is the glue that holds this messy media system together.

Now What?

The following concepts are so fundamental to how the media work today, that we will label them the "Five Global Truths" that help to explain a messy media world.

> **Truth #1: Convergence**
> **Truth #2: Symbiosis**
> **Truth #3: Circuits**
> **Truth #4: Brands**
> **Truth #5: Economics**

For some, the word "truth" may be too strong of a word. You may associate it with rigid thinking or a set of irrefutable laws. If that's the case, then think of these Global Truths as a compass with five points to help you navigate these messy and highly exciting times in the media world.

In the coming chapters, we'll explore each truth individually and in detail. And, while each of the Five Global Truths is its own force, they also influence each other. We'll see how the Five Global Truths are all coming together to create one stunning big picture.

An exciting media world awaits those who are willing to embrace these new truths. In the coming chapters, we will see how leveraging these new ways of looking at the media can generate new energy and success. We will meet some of the pioneers whose early actions helped to illuminate these truths. And we will discuss the challenges faced by the media and marketers who are trying to adjust to these new forces. The road for some won't be easy. But with a new vision and a few simple truths, we can all thrive in a messy media world.

CHAPTER FOUR

GLOBAL TRUTH #1
CONVERGENCE

Convergence (n.): the merging of distinct technologies, industries or devices into a unified whole.

(Source: Merriam-webster.com).

TRUTH: Media used to be separate and distinct. In the digital age, they started converging, becoming similar in function and form. An industry that was built around individual media channels will need to tear down those divisions and instead prepare for the convergence of all media onto digital screens. Welcome to the Screen Democracy!

Here's a Buzzword That's Truly Buzz-Worthy

Convergence is a hot buzzword, and deservedly so! What can this book possibly illuminate about the topic of convergence that you, the reader, don't already know? And why is this phenomenon the first Global Truth that can explain media chaos?

The answer is quite simple: we used to operate in a world where the media were separate and distinct. We built an entire industry, along with business models and marketing practices,that treated each medium as its own entity. We created the irrefutable laws of media dynamics that factored effects one medium at a time.

Now the media are coming together. The old models simply don't fit a convergence paradigm. Our thinking and our practices need to catch up. We need to come together to find holistic solutions.

Media Used to Be Fundamentally Different

To readers who don't distinguish much between their television, their laptop, their tablet or their mobile phone, this entire chapter may seem completely out of touch. But we have to deal with the reality that our existing systems and thinking are left over from a time when media were fundamentally different. Media convergence simply didn't exist.

During the Newtonian Media Era, and even during the Era of Media Relativity, media used to be distinct from one another. Technology platforms were different. Content was different. Different media served different needs. We talked on telephones. We listened to the radio. We read printed pages of newspapers and magazines. And we used the computer as a "lean forward" device to seek out a universe of information that lived on the internet. Stop and think about how different things were not too long ago: the only personal medium that served up video content was your television!

Back Then, We Could Target Audiences by their Media Consumption Patterns

In this world, each medium had unique strengths. Some media were known for building audience reach while others were better for message frequency. And we could plan various combinations of media (i.e., the media mix) based on media quintiles: groups of audiences categorized by their media consumption patterns. Some consumers tended to be heavy users of one particular medium and light users of others. By combining media and creating a mix, we could manipulate target audience reach and frequency in order to deliver the desired outcome.

That was then, and this is now. Media convergence is manifesting in an important way: almost every medium now comes with a screen. Why is this happening now?

TECHNOLOGY

Digital technology changed media in profound ways. Every medium imaginable now has some form of a digital structure to it. Digital used to be reserved for computers, but now every medium is either completely digital or has a digital offering. That means the basic technological structure of all media is now more similar than dissimilar.

How did this structure manifest? Nearly every medium today has a screen interface. Suddenly, communication modalities that never involved a screen are being delivered on screen devices. Printed words, pictures, music and our conversations have become the domain of screens. Historically, screen devices were used to consume video formats exclusively. Today, as long as content is digitized, it can land on a screen.

Does this mean that video has lost its importance? Quite the opposite is true. We are now in the midst of a video democracy where any media company with some form of digital distribution platform can enter the video business. Consumers of all ages are watching more video on more screens than ever before. Video is the common denominator and any media company can have a piece of the pie.

Media Laws Don't Work the Way They Used To

How will this new screen democracy affect the old-world laws of media effects? Will media still accumulate effects the same way? These old-school laws are still taught in our classrooms and practiced out in the marketplace. But they don't seem to work quite the way they used to. The media world is experiencing its own version of warp physics. Some basic tenants we accepted as true are now true in reverse.

The laws of media effects explore tradeoffs between target audience "reach" and "frequency." Reach refers to the estimated number of target audience members exposed at least one time to a message. Frequency refers to the average of number of times the target audience is exposed to the message. Prevailing wisdom was to build a media mix to reach as many people as possible at an appropriate frequency level that would reinforce the message without crossing the line into annoyance and message wear-out.

"Reach" Is Now "Frequency"

Thanks to the screen democracy, what used to be "reach" is now "frequency." Not so long ago, we needed to use a combination of media formats (i.e., multimedia mix) to reach a broad consumer demographic with our marketing messages. Why? Because we used to see a significant divide in media consumption between the digital media natives and the rest of us. Media quintile data illustrated clear patterns of media preference: certain demographic cohorts were heavy users of one medium and light to non-users of others. The media mix was therefore crucial to ensure that "everyone" saw the brand's message.

Not anymore. We have mounting evidence that all consumers—both digital media natives and "immigrants"—are consuming vast amounts of all media. There are no longer tradeoffs. Consumers simply add a new screen to their repertoire and keep all the rest. We're just spending more time interacting with more screens! This has a profound impact on the role of media mix. All of a sudden, a multimedia mix is driving frequency along with reach.

This reversal of media effects (reach is now frequency) has profound implications for how we think about and schedule video communications. If the same piece of video communication—let's say a television commercial or some variant of the commercial—appears on multiple screen devices such as a television, a laptop, a tablet and/or a mobile phone, we can expect the video to wear out (lose its communication appeal) very quickly. The accumulation of screens may drive frequency of exposure and commercial fatigue to new heights.

How Do We Measure This New Reality?

Media audience measurement systems have to catch up to this new reality; otherwise, the calculations of cross-screen reach and frequency will remain flawed. In order to put reach and frequency back into their proper perspectives, we need an audience measurement method that captures the behavior of individuals as they interact with and across *all* their screens.

While the race is on among major media audience measurement firms to find a solution, the transition from single device measurement to cross-device measurement is proving to be very difficult and very costly. We're still left in chaos: Our ability to accurately measure what is truly going on in this new blended world of screens remains a bit of a mystery. As we will learn in the coming pages of this book, that mystery may be best left unsolved. There are bigger opportunities awaiting us.

PIONEERS

Who were the pioneers in media convergence? First and foremost, we have to give Apple the credit it is due. This brand, singlehandedly, understood the power and attraction of a brilliantly designed digital screen and gave us product innovation that changed the face of every device imaginable.

Apple Rethinks Screens

Apple made us rethink what screen devices could be used for. It introduced the idea that a personal computer could be used for more than left-brain pursuits. With the suite of creative tools that was standard on every Mac, we could use our computers to fuel the right sides of our brains as well.

With the launch of the iPhone, Apple transformed mobile phones from talking and messaging devices into "the internet in our pockets." And, although Microsoft launched the first tablet computer nearly a decade before, Apple realized that the tablet was more than a smaller, less functional computer. They re-imagined the device to blend the screen worlds of work and play.

Quite simply, we would not be experiencing convergence today without Apple's foresight to shift our mindsets toward our screen devices. They made us ready and willing to pick up any device available to fulfill any host of wants and needs.

We Can Consume the Same Content Across All Devices

While rethinking screens was an important first step in the journey toward convergence, something else even more profound had to happen: the content that we consumed on one device needed to become seamlessly available across all our devices. Apple had the brilliant foresight to make this happen as well. Since Apple used the same basic operating system for all of its devices, consumers could simply pick up the nearest iPhone or MacBook and consume the same content wherever, whenever, and however they chose.

Once the same content could be consumed on any digital device, we were able to tear down the silos that used to confine content to a specific channel. Today, the idea of screen neutrality has become second-nature. We simply pick up the most conveniently accessible screen device and consume digital content to our heart's content. By tearing down the silos across their own screen devices, Apple shaped an entirely new media experience: one that we call media convergence.

Legacy Media Evolves

While Apple was busy synchronizing digital screens, legacy media companies that were historically confined to specific modes of distribution began to break out of their silos. They began to distribute content in digital formats that could be consumed on and across all these screen devices.

To today's reader, this may seem like such an obvious thing to do. But stop and think about the legacy of most media channels: their distribution used to define them. Literally! Newspapers had the word "paper" ingrained in their identities. In television, we used to distinguish between "broadcast" and "cable" networks simply because some networks were around when signals were broadcast over-the-air while others were formed in the era of cable distribution. And the term "website" quite literally referred to a specific "site" on the Worldwide Web. When your industry is named according to your legacy, it's no small feat to venture beyond the boundaries of your original channel. However, in the late aughts of this century, nearly every sector within the media ecosystem did just that.

Each of the changes described below could fill the pages of its own book! My goal is to provide you with a quick snapshot of the profound shifts in each legacy sector during relatively the same time period that screens themselves were transforming (circa 2007 to date). Television became "TV Everywhere." Radio leaked off the airwaves and onto our phones. Magazines became as visually arresting on an iPad as they were in glossy stock. And newspapers discovered that news without "paper" was a new reality—one that required a new business model.

Television Becomes "TV Everywhere"

How did television become "TV Everywhere?" A few bold broadcast networks (NBC, Fox and Disney shortly thereafter) decided to take control of their destiny in this new landscape by launching Hulu. While the naysayers may have called Hulu "Clown Co." in its early days, Hulu quickly grew as a mainstream distribution alternative for television. Hulu knew that it would shake up the television industry by "beaming television content directly to your portable computing device" (Hulu Super Bowl commercial, February 2009). In the same commercial, Hulu called itself "An evil plot to destroy the world."

As it turned out, the world would be just fine. In fact, it arguably got even better when television content became available for consumption on any screen device. The only "world" that was in trouble was that of cable and satellite distributors, who had been charging consumers high subscription fees for years. Once Hulu (and other television streaming services like it) became a viable alternative, consumers began cancelling their cable and satellite subscriptions (known in the industry as "Cord Cutting").

In response, cable and satellite distributors had no

choice but to take a hard look at their businesses. Several cable operators launched "TV Everywhere" initiatives that allowed subscribers to view television content on any device with internet access. While cable and satellite television still needed to figure out its pricing model, they had at least begun to tear down the silo that kept television locked onto a specific channel.

Now, add Netflix to the mix. At the same time as "TV Everywhere" and Hulu gained popularity, Netflix expanded from a DVD-by-mail business to an online streaming service. Netflix began acquiring libraries of television content that its subscribers could view on any screen device, without commercial interruptions. This would prove to be a real game-changer, for both the distribution of television and the economics behind it.

Television would never be the same. Once distributed over the airwaves or through a cable conduit, TV was now showing up just about everywhere. Suddenly, consumers were watching video on every screen imaginable both with and without commercial interruptions.

Radio Leaks Off the Airwaves

When we analyze radio's journey through media convergence, we would be remiss if we didn't first dial back (pun intended) to August 1, 1981: the day MTV launched. By its very name, MTV (Music Television) epitomized the convergence of two historically separate broadcast media—radio and television—long before media convergence became a broad topic of conversation.

When MTV first launched, there were concerns that video would usurp radio, damaging the music industry. In fact, the song title of one of the first music videos to air on MTV, "Video Killed the Radio Star," played off this concern. Nothing could have been further from the truth. Instead, we learned that music is a universal cultural language that can suit any medium.

Even more surprising, MTV was not the primary pioneer in the music convergence movement. Instead, the true pioneer in transforming music from the airwaves to all platforms was Apple. When Apple launched the iPhone in 2007, they had the foresight to place iTunes directly onto its phones.

This could have signaled the end of radio as we knew it. Instead of listening to radio over-the-air, people started listening to their personal music libraries whenever and wherever their iPhones traveled with them. However, radio broadcasters did not remain idle. Instead, they harnessed the same technology that enabled iTunes to live on an iPhone. With it, they created applications (Apps) that allowed radio stations to be "streamed" on digital devices.

Meanwhile, internet-based music platforms such as Pandora and Spotify began to take off. These services blended the best of radio with the best of iTunes. Instead of having to buy songs and create playlists, these services offered subscribers access to huge listening libraries and an abundance of playlists that became smarter over time based upon individual listening patterns. These streaming services became so popular that Apple responded with its own version: Apple Music.

So where does all this transformation leave the radio industry today? Radio has grown far beyond the confines of the AM/FM broadcast spectrum to become a major force in audio communication in both terrestrial and digital formats. What once required a radio in order to "tune in" can now be enjoyed on any digital device.

Magazines Meet Screens

While most major magazines had websites for years, they were often treated as an afterthought by editors and publishers who had a "print-first" mindset. In many publishing houses, digital was the poor stepchild who didn't receive the time, attention or resources they deserved.

All that changed during the Apple screen revolution, especially once tablets became mainstream. With tablets, magazine editors saw the potential for a screen experience that could complement the visual beauty and engaging reading experience that magazine-style editorial commands. At the end of 2009, *The New York Times* published the story, "Magazines Get Ready for Tablets." And, just two short years after, most major publishing houses were on board.

By the end of 2011, Time Inc. had announced that all 21 of its major US titles would have tablet editions. At the same time, Hearst announced the opening of its App Lab, and Meredith announced tablet editions of its flagship brands, *Better Homes and Gardens*, *Parents*, and *Fitness*. And, while Condé Nast put the brakes on its tablet efforts in 2011, their reticence was short-lived. Not only has Condé Nast joined the ranks of other major publishers in embracing digital distribution, they have boldly shuttered the print editions of some of their younger-skewing titles (such as *Teen Vogue* and *Self*).

Fast-forward to today and nearly every successful magazine brand has a digital version. And those magazine websites that were once ignored? They are now rich content hubs that are screen optimized for desktop and mobile. Many now offer video storytelling and accept video advertising. What was once a medium of glossy paper stock has evolved into a collection of media brands that can be accessed on paper, on screens, or even both.

Newspapers Face New Competition

What happens when you separate the "paper" from the news? All of a sudden, you're met with a stark reality: Paper is slow and expensive to produce while with the emergence of the internet, "news" is immediate and everywhere. Newspapers were suddenly met with new forms of competition from all corners of the media ecosystem. Convergence took away the geographic boundaries that used to insulate many newspapers from significant competition.

Granted, most newspapers had their own websites well before media convergence was truly realized. Technically, each newspaper's digital footprint reached as far and wide as any new competition from elsewhere in the media ecosystem. However, these websites weren't the main focus of the enterprise, nor were they generating much revenue. The main source of focus and income came from the paper, itself.

All that changed once Craigslist, an online classified advertising portal, gained popularity. Classified advertising revenue used to be the lifeblood of local newspapers. Once that revenue went away, newspapers were left with a daunting task. They had to plug this massive financial hole while figuring out a way to make money from their digital offerings. Could newspapers slow the forces of convergence and erect paywalls around their digital content? Or would they become the first fatality of this new media world, countering this author's belief that no medium will be single-handedly destroyed by another?

National newspaper brands such as *The Wall Street Journal* and *The New York Times* are living proof that newspapers can thrive among all the competition caused by media convergence. Perhaps these brands are showing us the way because they were always valued more for the strength of their content product—their brand of journalism per se—than for their distribution footprint.

The Wall Street Journal was a true pioneer. They built a digital business long before anyone in the industry had a sense of the true potential of online media. *The Wall Street Journal*'s digital paywall dates all the way back to 1997 and today, 50 percent of the paper's total circulation is digital. We'll hear more about this pioneering paper when we get to Truth #5: Economics.

Another national newspaper powerhouse, *The New York Times*, has been aggressively building its digital enterprise. Over the past decade, *The New York Times* has been experimenting with various iterations of online paywalls. And while there is an ongoing debate whether the paywall is successful, no one disputes that the newspaper's audience has grown far beyond the boundaries of its printed product. As of the first quarter of 2018, *The New York Times* boasts 2.8 million subscribers to its digital editions.

The ride may be bumpy, but newspapers who can truly stand for something once the boundaries of fixed distribution are stripped away will still play a role in this new media landscape. We are witnessing a classic tale of "Survival of the Fittest"—one of the oldest themes in any evolutionary journey.

Digital Gets a Facelift

Convergence clearly and forever changed the face of legacy media as we knew it. It fundamentally changed digital media as well. With the exception of YouTube, most digital media experiences were limited to mainly text and some visuals. To illustrate this point, take a journey through your Facebook posts from the early days to today and you will see the transition for yourself. Facebook was simply evolving in reverse: it was converging to look more like older, more "traditional" media.

Some of you may recall when online "portals" such as AOL and Yahoo were known mainly as email providers and search engines. We used to type text into search boxes on their home pages and we would be rewarded with a text listing of web addresses that would link us to informative content. Today, the front pages of AOL and Yahoo don't look much different than the front page of any major news or entertainment brand's website.

Even YouTube looks much different today thanks to convergence. YouTube has evolved from a user-generated video content portal into its own destination for high-quality television programming. YouTube recently announced the launch of YouTube TV: a subscription streaming service that will carry both libraries of television content as well as live "event" fare. YouTube TV launched in a big way: baseball fans could watch the 2017 MLB World Series on either the Fox Broadcast Network or on YouTube! When America's pastime (for you baseball fans) can be streamed on YouTube, you know that convergence has truly arrived!

Today, digital media brands can offer the same rich content experiences that used to be available only on televisions, on radios, or in the printed pages of newspapers and magazines. The best content experience wins. It doesn't matter whether a media brand started as an "analog" brand or a "digital" brand. They all compete in the same space and they all offer similar content experiences.

TRAVELING THROUGH CHAOS

Both media companies and marketers are having a difficult time letting go of the media silos left over from a previous era. Why do those old silos hold so much power? It all comes down to money: how media companies make money and how marketers spend money.

Why Would We Trade Dollars for Pennies?

Back in 2008, Jeff Zucker, who was at the time head of NBC Universal, gave a speech with a line that has since become famous in media circles. Jeff spoke of "…trading analog dollars for digital pennies." Media companies made a lot more money from their legacy platforms than from their digital platforms. When asked five years later, Jeff Zucker, now the President of CNN, revised his forecast to "…dimes and even quarters."

Perhaps if you asked him today, Jeff would be more optimistic. But it is highly unlikely that he would say that digital media now generates digital dollars. For a host of reasons that can fill their own book, the legacy media business was more profitable. And, even though most media companies today make money from both their legacy channels and their new channels, there is still quite a bit of profit remaining in those old silos. Therefore, many media companies are slowing the growth from analog to digital intentionally to hang onto those profits for as long as they can.

Media Companies Create Scarcity Around Content

How do media companies fight the forces of convergence? It all comes down to content. While advances in technology make it easy for the same piece of content to show up just about everywhere, most content is contained to a specific destination based upon distribution rights and royalties.

When a media company produces its own content, they are going to distribute that content in ways that enable it to make the most money. The revenue comes from a couple key sources:

audience subscriber fees and/or advertising revenue. Once revenue is maximized in the most highly profitable channel, the media company redistributes that content onto other, less profitable channels.

When a media company does not produce their own content and instead they pay rights fees to syndicate content from a third party producer, they are going to negotiate terms that limit the content from showing up elsewhere. This provides the media company with a better opportunity to earn a return on their investment in high quality content.

In essence, media companies try to create scarcity around their content product: both their own content and the content they syndicate from other content producers. Remember the laws of supply and demand. If audience demand for high quality content can be steered toward fewer destinations for consuming that content, media companies can earn more money. There is an economic incentive to keep those silos up despite the forces of convergence that strive to tear them down.

Marketers Are Stuck with the Reality of Business and Finance Silos

While many marketers understand the forces of convergence and are shifting their mindsets toward "integrated marketing communications," they are stuck with the reality of marketing finance. Advertising is considered an expense on the balance sheet. Consequently, each expense must be carefully managed and ultimately attributable to some measure of return-on-investment. This forces marketers away from the big picture of convergence. Until we can create a new system of marketing finance that rewards holistic thinking, we will continue to prop up those walls that should ultimately come down.

Even if we tear down the walls created by marketing finance, we are left with a marketing services industry that is highly fractured. When media were separate and distinct from one another, it made sense for agencies to specialize in specific pieces of the marketing function. Now, we have to put the pieces back together.

Who is best equipped to develop truly integrated marketing communications? Is it a traditional advertising agency? Is it a digital advertising agency? Should a public relations agency take the lead? Is it a new breed of agency that doesn't exist today? Or are the media companies themselves best equipped to help marketers develop content for a new media world? This is a big problem. No one wants to put themselves out of business. The journey toward truly integrated marketing services will be painful and casualties will be unavoidable.

With All These Screens, Our Messages Are Overwhelming Consumers

Regardless of *who* creates marketing content and *how* it is funded, one thing is certain: convergence requires that we rethink what we ultimately place on all those screens. In many cases, marketers take advertising content created for legacy media and then adjust it to fit the technical specifications of the screen. This approach isn't working all that well. Consumer acceptance of advertising in digital media is extremely low and many are downloading ad blockers.

Why is there such a low tolerance for the same or similar ads in new spaces? If the marketing message stays relatively the same across multiple formats, we will create far too much message frequency. Remember, thanks to media convergence, the laws of reach and frequency are no longer clear. If we simply place the same content across multiple screens, we'll burn out!

We Need to Figure out How to Measure Convergence—ASAP

How extensive is this burn out? We really don't know. Audience measurement has not yet caught up to the reality of convergence. For the most part, measurement is still stuck in silos. Major players such as Nielsen and comScore are racing to provide holistic measurement of individuals across their devices. Unfortunately, this is easier said than done. Measuring audiences across all their devices requires samples of prolific size that are extremely expensive and do not fully capture the audiences of every media brand on every media channel.

To make matters worse, we tend to measure audiences differently across media channels. Television audiences have, historically, been measured based upon "opportunities to see." Digital media, on the other hand, is typically evaluated by some measure of consumer behavior such as a "click." Until we reconcile these discrepancies and find a way to increase sample sizes we will be left in the dark regarding the true measure of media convergence.

Despite all the challenges that convergence presents for the media business, media companies and marketers have no choice but to figure it out and do so quickly. Consumers have fully embraced media convergence and they will continue to fuel its forward momentum. For them, media convergence opens up a whole new world where content is seamlessly available across multiple screens.

Consumer adoption is so prolific that a recent research study found that half of consumers no longer refer to a television device when they say, "I'm watching television." The majority of consumers are now platform agnostic. They consume content on the most convenient screen available to them. This ship has sailed and both media companies and marketers need to catch up.

TRUTH

While convergence is wreaking havoc with old business models, there is a wealth of potential waiting for both media companies and marketers who can embrace this phenomenon. Media companies can expand well beyond the boundaries of their originating channel to provide compelling content wherever, whenever and however their audiences prefer.

Sure, there will be more competition once they lose the protection of silos. But there will be far more opportunity as well. As media companies expand beyond their originating channels, chances are new audiences will discover them along the way. More audience means more revenue, whether it's subscription-based or advertising-based or both.

Convergence will also have a profound and positive influence on integrated marketing communications once marketers strip away the old, channel-based approach to setting budgets and developing marketing plans. Convergence eliminates the need for developing marketing strategies one channel at a time.

Instead, marketers will be able to focus on new priorities: making the content great and empowering consumers to accelerate content far and wide. This is what we meant by the reordering of the three Cs that we discussed earlier in the text. Convergence makes it possible to shift emphasis away from individual channels and onto more important things such as engaging consumers with compelling content.

So What Should We Do About This Whole "Platform Agnostic" Thing?

In order to fully embrace convergence, we must take the idea of "platform agnostic" from a buzzword to a practical reality. This is easier said than done. So let's break this idea down into more bite-sized actions:

1. First and foremost, media have to embrace their own convergence. If more media companies create engaging content experiences on their second and third screen platforms without treating them like stepchildren, the revenue will follow.

Speaking of revenue, there is more advertising revenue on the horizon for media companies who become transmedia brands. While advertising revenue may shift from one part of the ecosystem to another, a great, platform agnostic media brand can easily compete for that revenue. In the future, media companies must build their identities outside of the channels that originally defined them and instead create truly platform agnostic, transmedia brands.

2. Audience measurement has to catch up. We need to continuously refresh our reach and frequency models to ensure that the most up-to-date, multiscreen behavior is represented in our media plans. This requires a holistic, single source view of media consumption across multiple screen devices. It means that we will have to spend more money on larger research panels and we're going to have to agree on a common measure that works for all these devices.

We aren't going to be able to measure everything. And that is going to have to be okay. Media audience research was always an estimate: a proxy for building models. As we deal with more data that is generated by audience behavior in digital media, we cannot lose sight of the big picture. We are going to need to put aside discrete measures of audience behavior on specific channels to ensure that our view of audience behavior is whole. That's what convergence is all about.

3. Marketers need to change the way they set media budgets. Advertising budgets need to break free from old media

silos that no longer exist. This will be difficult because the market mix models that so many marketers rely on to help measure their return on investments are built one media channel at a time. Instead of focusing on single channel attribution, we are going to have to learn to model the big picture. This means giving brand managers and their agencies more flexibility to shift advertising budgets across historically sacred lines.

4. Last, marketers will need to abandon the current practice of hiring separate agencies to craft specific messages for supposedly separate channels. On the flip side, marketers will have to resist the temptation to place existing advertisements in every medium they can.

Marketers and their agencies will need to collaborate with media companies to create new forms of marketing content that can engage audiences across their devices. Old advertising formats don't work well in new media environments. Convergence will enable us to reimagine what is possible if marketers, their agencies, and the media themselves are willing to design a new playbook.

It Won't Be Easy!

Embracing the forces of convergence won't be easy. There are still obstacles we need to face as we attempt to tear down those old media silos. Luckily, we have four additional global truths that will help us on the way. Each force that is shaping the new media landscape works with the others to present new opportunities in this new media world. By learning and embracing these truths, we can remove the barriers that still exist and truly celebrate the exponential potential that awaits us.

CHAPTER FIVE

GLOBAL TRUTH #2
SYMBIOSIS

Symbiosis (n): the living together in more or less intimate association or close union of two dissimilar organisms, a cooperative relationship.

(Source: Merriam-webster.com)

> *TRUTH: While doomsayers would have you believe that digital media will destroy its analog predecessors, evidence doesn't support a story of "winners and losers." Sure, there will be individual casualties. But centuries of evidence suggests 'new' media make 'old' media better. When we practice transmedia storytelling, consumers can use combinations of media across channels to engage with stories.*

We Have the "Hunter" and "Gatherer" Story All Wrong

We are a species of hunters and gatherers. It's how we're wired. We hunt prey that fall beneath us in the food chain, and we gather materials to help us thrive. Both actions are essential to our lives. But, for some reason, we focus on the "hunter" part of the equation; we tend to forget the "gatherer" side of things. When we look at the systems in our world, we quickly try to figure out the food chain. What sits on top? What is going to get killed off? We expect to see winners and losers.

We rarely talk about the cornucopia of "stuff" that we collect to help us survive and thrive. Perhaps there's more drama in focusing on the kill, and it's less interesting on the surface to consider the strange relationships that emerge from the things we gather in our lives. Such is the story with modern media consumption. We tend to gather an entire market basket of media to help us survive and thrive in our daily lives. Something new comes along, and we gather it up. Instead of letting go of anything, we simply make more room in our repertoire.

What are we left with? More hours of media consumption than the total number of hours in an actual day! And the only way this phenomenon can happen is if the media work with, as opposed to against, each other.

TECHNOLOGY

While in the previous chapter we could point to digitization of all media as the catalyst for the first global truth, convergence, there really is no technology story that can explain the phenomenon of symbiosis. Rather, the phenomenon is driven by human behavior. When a new medium comes along, we simply make room for it, and we create a new role for the existing medium. Skeptical?

Make Room for More Media Because Nothing Is Going Away

Let's go all the way back to Gutenberg's printing press. This transformative invention forever changed the face of communication. So why, approximately 300 years after the invention of Gutenberg's printing press, did Paul Revere make his infamous midnight ride? Why did town criers still exist? While the value of the printed page was critical, it could not replace or displace the value of one of the oldest forms of human communication: word of mouth.

Even today, word of mouth is still one of the most influential modes of media and message delivery. The more things change, the more they stay the same. While the examples outlined in the pages of this book are far removed from Gutenberg's printing press and Paul Revere's famous ride, the lesson is still the same. Make room for more media: nothing is going away.

We Keep Waiting for Winners and Losers, but It Just Doesn't Happen

Let's fast-forward from Revolutionary War times to the 20th century. During the 20th century, media changed to a degree we had never experienced before. Suddenly, we had an unprecedented number of choices. If you look at a 20th century timeline of media innovation, you will be struck by the growth in channels without the demise of others. Think about it. Can you recall a single media industry that has completely collapsed?

True, formats have changed and several media properties have come and gone. That's going to happen. But what we are talking about here is the foundational structure of the media. It just keeps growing! And the only way such growth can be sustained is through symbiosis.

Enter the dawn of the 21st century. Despite the history lessons of the 20th century, doomsayers have been filling headlines with predictions that "old" media will be displaced by "new" media. Why are we talking about the fall of old media? What is happening now that makes us believe that centuries of media cohabitation will suddenly change? The idea that media is divided into winners and losers doesn't hold water. It never did.

If You Need Proof, Just Look at Television and YouTube

Think of YouTube and the other "tube"...television. YouTube launched back in 2005 as an internet forum for creative self-expression. Hence, the tagline: "Broadcast Yourself." Some of the old guard broadcasters feared that YouTube would steal the time and attention of their audiences. In reality, something quite different happened.

Instead of audiences abandoning high quality, high production value television content, they actually started uploading this content onto YouTube—oftentimes illegally. So, what did the broadcasters do? One in particular, Viacom, waged war on YouTube. In 2007, they filed a copyright infringement suit to safeguard against the illegal distribution of their valuable content.

While Viacom was fighting the battles to protect intellectual property from illegal distribution, others quickly realized YouTube's incredible potential. Broadcasters themselves began to upload memorable scenes from their programs onto YouTube. Advertisers started uploading their television commercial content onto YouTube (for free, by the way).

In response, consumers began to engage with this content in a host of ways: through "likes," "shares," "comments" and, at times, even uploading their own parodies of all this content. In essence, YouTube created a second creative ecosystem for television and the advertisers that supported it.

Ultimately, YouTube became a free marketing arm of the television industry. It served as a highly effective sampling mechanism for television content. And, while it was attracting new audiences to TV shows, it also became a destination where existing fans of TV shows could engage with their favorite clips and outtakes. YouTube helped build audience size and audience loyalty to popular TV programs—without the hefty expense of audience "tune-in" campaigns.

On the flipside, what did television bring to YouTube in the early days? Television filled an important content inventory need for YouTube. While the channel was built as a broadcast conduit for user-generated content, this form of self-expression proved to be quite difficult to monetize. Users weren't paying to watch YouTube and advertisers were reticent to buy advertising adjacent to user-generated content due to quality and brand safety concerns.

As more television content landed on YouTube, the channel could offer advertisers a safer environment for their messages. Since YouTube earns its revenue primarily from the sale of advertising, this unintended landing spot for television content helped to pave the way for YouTube's financial survival.

Why was there such a disconnect between the perception that YouTube was a threat to television and the reality that YouTube and television actually thrive in a symbiotic relationship? It all goes back to our misguided hunter mentality. We expected one medium to land on top of the food chain—at the expense of the other.

While our thinking was misguided, our gatherer behavior saved the day. Just as the town crier could still exist in harmony with the printing press, we found a way to add YouTube to our already rich market basket of media experiences. We learned that there was plenty of room to "Broadcast Yourself" and still celebrate the power and influence of "Broadcast Television."

Symbiosis Leads to a New Kind of Storytelling

In order for media channels to work together in symbiosis, audiences need to be rewarded for their time and engagement across multiple channels. If they experience the same or similar content over and over again, they will likely burn out.

Remember, thanks to the forces of convergence, message fatigue can now easily happen. The same content can be experienced across multiple screens unless we do something about it. Audiences need to experience something new in each channel that adds to their understanding and/or their enjoyment of content that they've engaged with elsewhere. This form of narrative development is called transmedia storytelling.

PIONEERS

While many media companies were desperately trying to hang onto the past, a few bold pioneers realized that their existing and emerging channels could work together in symbiosis. These pioneers embraced transmedia storytelling as a means of managing the flow of audiences on and across different channels. The early pioneers tended to place the most important piece of a transmedia story on the legacy channel that accounted for the majority of its revenue. And, at the time, it made sense for them to do so.

Meanwhile, they quickly became adept at building ancillary content on emerging channels that could serve two very important goals. First, the ancillary content rewarded loyal audiences for their time, attention and willingness to cross channels to gain a deeper level of involvement with the transmedia story. Next, this ancillary content became a sampling mechanism for new audiences who, once engaged, proved more than willing to travel back to the legacy platform for more.

Thanks to symbiosis, these media pioneers discovered that they could expand their franchises onto emerging platforms without having to give up their legacies. There were truly no winners and losers in the mix.

Time Makes a Bold Move

Time magazine understood this phenomenon. In 2007, it made a bold move to capitalize upon the symbiosis between the print magazine and online news sources. On January 5 of that year, *Time* issued its first Friday publication. This was a provocative departure from the newsweekly standard publication day, Monday. In a letter to his readership issued the following day, Managing Editor Richard Stengel shared this rationale: "The new publication date reflects the way the Internet is affecting pretty much everything about the news business. Today, our print magazine and TIME.com are complementary halves of the Time brand."

Stengel and his team understood that the weekend offers a time for reflection. The print magazine could serve its readers best by shifting its publication day to Friday. Let the internet own the harried workweek and let the print publication own a weekend for reflection and agenda setting. The two media channels could now better support and reinforce each other.

Obviously, *Time* was onto something. The brand was able to grow its digital footprint through its robust website and multiple social media platforms while still circulating approximately 3 million copies of its printed magazine every week.

HBO Deepens Storytelling Across Screens

At the same time that *Time* announced this bold move, television content producers also began to explore how multiple screens could deepen what was, otherwise, a "broadcast" experience. HBO proved itself to be an especially innovative network.

In 2007, HBO created the "Voyeur" project in support of its on-demand movie *The Watcher*. This bold experiment turned the outside of an apartment building in New York City into a screen to portray various vignettes to "voyeurs" on the city streets. The experience was enhanced online through webisodes that provided rich back stories on each character vignette that appeared on the building. Ultimately, the on-demand movie *The Watcher* told the tale of what happens when a voyeur witnesses a murder through an apartment window.

The experience was truly exponential in terms of the audience it reached and engaged. HBO understood that each new screen that it used to tell pieces of the story enhanced the overall experience for the viewer and created a deeper level of engagement for the broadcast experience.

Broadcast "Dinosaurs" Expand Storytelling, Too

While HBO is known for pushing the envelope to create and tell powerful stories, it was not alone in the early days of the transmedia storytelling movement. Broadcast networks, who are often referred to as the "dinosaurs" of the media industry, quickly caught on and began to leverage multiple screens to create immersive content experiences for their fans. Each of the major networks had a pioneering success story: ABC's *Lost* (2004-2010), CBS's *Survivor* (2000-Present), Fox's *American Idol* (2002-2016) and NBC's *Heroes* (2006-2010) are all prime examples of the transmedia storytelling format in broadcast television.

One of the Oldest Advertisers Around Throws Away the Rule Book

Many of today's marketers are still scratching their heads trying to figure out how to fit all these media into the mix. So it's a little ironic that Procter & Gamble, one of the oldest advertisers around, took the lead in leveraging symbiotic media relationships. Its Old Spice brand showed just how tightly linked social networks and video-serving media truly are.

Back in 2010, Procter & Gamble and its agency Wieden + Kennedy found themselves in an enviable position. Their new television commercial for Old Spice Body Wash became wildly popular. The commercial, known as "The Man Your Man Could Smell Like," prompted all kinds of cultural buzz around the ideal fantasy man (who smelled great thanks to Old Spice). Everyone from celebrities such as Oprah to "besties" on social media were envisioning their own versions of the infamous man riding his white horse in the iconic commercial.

Instead of passively letting this cultural buzz run its course, P&G and their agency leaned into the opportunity. They invited "fans" to create their own scenarios and share them on social media. The agency then selected over 180 different fan-generated fantasies and professionally produced them as the next generation of narrative in the fantasy. These special vignettes populated an entire YouTube channel that delighted consumers and deepened engagement with the Old Spice brand. The results pushed both brand conversations and sales to exponential heights.

The case—and everyone associated with it—deserved every bit of the hype and attention it received. Why? Because it demonstrated what is truly possible when a marketer is willing to throw away the old rule books and create an interactive, multimedia experience that considers how consumers actually use media.

Could anyone accurately predict the potential exposures from this campaign with any certainty? Absolutely not! But the consumer behavior was there, so P&G and Wieden acted. And let's not forget the popular television commercial that started the whole thing. Once again, we had evidence that great content, even in a form as traditional as a television commercial, could fuel a transmedia story across media channels.

Fans Send Betty White on a Journey from the Super Bowl to SNL

While media companies and marketers were struggling to break out of their silos, consumers were taking matters into their own hands. In one now famous case, consumers actually pulled marketers and media companies right along with them. Consider the "Betty White" phenomenon. What started as a great casting decision for a Snickers Super Bowl commercial turned into a pop culture firestorm that led to Betty White becoming the oldest ever host of *Saturday Night Live*.

It all began with a single airing of a 30-second Snickers commercial during the 2010 Super Bowl. In the ad, a young hipster guy playing football with his buddies morphs into Betty White (because he was playing like, you know, a 90-year-old woman). Betty White's cameo appearance in a pick-up football game was epic! The commercial drew rave reviews among the press and fans in the post-Super Bowl "ad-o-sphere."

Shortly thereafter, Betty White fans on Facebook started advocating for Betty White to host *Saturday Night Live*. The conversation quickly swelled into a movement, with both the mainstream press and the show's producers taking notice.

Ultimately, Betty White was announced as the host for *SNL's* Mother's Day episode. The May 8th broadcast was a smash success, drawing the highest audiences in the show's recent history. And the broadcast provided a perfect contextual frame for the re-airing of the original Snickers "Betty White" commercial.

Post-broadcast, the enthusiasm ensued, with people rushing online to watch clips of her monologue. Shortly after, NBC posted the entire episode on Hulu. It became one of the most viewed programs on Hulu at the time. These online video exposures created even more opportunities to air the original commercial. And the story continues.

The Betty White phenomenon could only happen because the media operated in symbiotic relationships. Each media platform played a critical role in the movement, reinforcing what unfolded on other media. If you took any medium out of the story, the whole movement would have collapsed!

In both the Old Spice and Snickers examples, the most traditional of advertising forms was the catalyst for these important, pioneering stories. Sorry to disappoint, but there was no battle of old vs. new media. There were no media winners and losers. Rather, both cases illustrate rich brand experiences that use what occurred on one media channel to create and enhance an experience in another.

TRAVELING THROUGH CHAOS

As we travel through media chaos, we are experiencing an interesting dichotomy. Whereas the media are aligning themselves into a new collaborative order, many industry pundits and marketers are still "hunting" for the winners and losers. There's a real perception vs. reality problem out there. Hopefully, as the evidence continues to build, we will be able to shift perceptions and begin to take advantage of the collaborative nature of media.

New Media and Legacy Media Make Each Other Better

Remember the story of YouTube and TV? Despite all the worry early on, YouTube turned out to be a great compliment to TV. As we fast-forward through media time we will discover that this pioneering love affair wasn't a fluke. Rather, most mainstream social media channels today are entwined with legacy media in some way. They make each other better. This is a far different scenario than the bleak picture painted by those who believe that increased time spent on social media means there's not much left for anything else. The reality of the situation is much more nuanced. Social media and legacy media work hand-in-hand.

What about the doomsayers' predictions that digital media would destroy its analog predecessors? Many were forecasting the wholesale demise of print media, namely magazines and newspapers. Guess what? They missed an important part of the narrative: legacy media could use digital to their own advantage as well. In fact, most legacy media have expanded onto digital channels themselves. And as more media franchises adopt transmedia storytelling, they are able to strengthen their content product and grow their total audience across channels.

Finally, perhaps the biggest drama waiting to unfold revolves around the television industry: all that star power, all that content and all that advertising revenue that's associated with it. Some industry 'experts' predicted that television would slowly die off as video moved onto the internet. Fast forward to today and nothing could be further from the truth. Instead, we are now entering a Second Golden Era of Television. Once again, there is proof that media are resilient.

Let's take a look...

The YouTube/TV Love Story Wasn't a Fluke

Let's revisit the pioneering story of YouTube vs TV. We now have evidence that supports what we first observed back when YouTube launched: YouTube and TV truly support each other. In August 2016, Adweek reported the results of a Nielsen study that was commissioned by YouTube's parent company, Google. The study found what we already suspected to be true: TV reach seems to drive YouTube engagement, and in turn, YouTube engagement drives TV reach.

Furthermore, all the early challenges that YouTube faced trying to monetize user-generated content are still plaguing the channel today. YouTube has recently come under fire for running advertising adjacent to illicit and downright dangerous content. Without high quality content from elsewhere in the media ecosystem, YouTube will continue to struggle to create a safe space for advertisers—and risk losing the advertising revenue it relies upon for its survival. The mutually beneficial, two-way street between YouTube and television is as apparent today as it was when YouTube first launched.

Twitter Storms Hit Legacy Media

Is the TV and YouTube love story a fluke? Not at all! As new social media channels emerge, we continue to see social media (of all kinds) go hand in hand with legacy media. For example, nearly every "important" event that unfolds on a legacy media channel immediately sparks what we now refer to as a "Twitter Storm."

These "Twitter Storms" are not a one-way street: We all know that the tweets of certain individuals—such as the President of the United States—serve as fodder that fills the airwaves and the pages of most legacy media. What would happen if you shut down the President's Twitter feed? The news media would scramble to fill its airwaves and pages, for sure!

While "Twitter Storms" have become second nature for us as consumers, they are also big business for media companies. Back in October 2013, Nielsen launched its "Twitter TV Ratings" service, which showed that Twitter engagement fuels TV ratings. Those TV ratings, in turn, fuel advertising revenue. Once Nielsen began to quantify the relationship between television audience engagement and tweet volume, many TV franchises began to actively promote engagement with their fans and followers on Twitter.

This is not just a television phenomenon: nearly every legacy media company today actively pursues this symbiotic relationship between its content and conversations about its content on Twitter. It's good for business! It drives audience engagement and, in turn, it drives revenue.

It's Time to Address the 200 Pound Social Media Gorilla

With both YouTube and Twitter under our belts, it's time to address the 200 pound social media gorilla: Facebook. You know, the great media vortex that's sucking up all of our time. Is it destroying legacy media in the process? Many pundits suggest that Facebook is to blame for the financial struggles of mainstream news media in the U.S. But ironically, it has become one of the best marketing assets for mainstream media in recent history! There's two main reasons for this.

First, Facebook is helping legacy media get their content out into the world. According to a 2017 survey by the Pew Research Center, approximately two-thirds of American adults get their news from social media (sometimes or often). And almost half of all American adults get at least some of their news from Facebook. Through Facebook, audiences have an opportunity to see trustworthy, legacy media content that otherwise might never reach them. Likewise, through "the power of share," Facebook helps content spread to new—and bigger—

audiences.

Second, because so many people get their news from Facebook, the aftershocks when the platform became tainted by "fake news" were felt far and wide. As a result of all the disinformation that was published on the platform—and others— leading up to the 2016 U.S. presidential election, we began to see renewed interest in legacy news media brands that had a strong reputation for reporting the truth. Once "fake news" started making headlines, subscriptions to highly respected brands like *The New York Times*, *The Washington Post*, and *The Wall Street Journal* soared. In an ironic twist, Facebook's own shortcomings may prove to be legacy media's savior.

Media Franchises Turn to Transmedia Storytelling to Fuel Growth

As we continue to travel through media chaos, we are discovering that franchises that embrace transmedia storytelling are realizing success. Just a few years ago, transmedia storytelling was considered an experimental narrative format. Today, it is the norm. Nearly every successful media franchise has figured out a way to present its narrative across multiple platforms to reward its audiences for their time, attention, and willingness to cross channels.

If You Think Print Media is Dying, Think Again

This new strategy is beginning to pay off. Just a few short years ago, doomsayers were ready to write off print media. Both magazines and newspapers were supposed to vanish and be replaced by new digital media formats. Yes print circulation is down. But it should decline for a simple reason: It's expensive. If a thriving transmedia brand has the opportunity to adjust its print/digital mix, it would be prudent to do so.

But declining print circulation and the decline of print

---

media brands are two very different things. According to the 2017 edition of the Magazine Media Factbook issued by the MPA (Association of Magazine Media), magazine brands actually grew their audience by an average of 6.4% in 2016 across all channels. These magazines are not simply trading audiences from one platform to the next. Rather, through enriching editorial experiences that draw audiences in and across channels, magazines are seeing audiences spend more and more time with their brands.

Newspapers are Catching On, Too

Magazines aren't the only legacy print media to embrace transmedia storytelling. Newspapers have caught on as well. Skeptical? Just check out *The Guardian*'s "Three Little Pigs" campaign, which turns the classic narrative inside out using print, video, and social media participation. You'll understand just how far beyond the printed page most newspapers are now willing to go.

Importantly, once print media break out beyond the boundaries of the page and expand their editorial footprint across other digital and social media channels, they can also compete for advertising revenue on these channels. It's great for storytelling and it's also great for business! How far can transmedia storytelling transform the print media industry? Grab your virtual reality headsets and join the *New York Times* to see a glimpse into the future.

Print Media Aren't the Only Transmedia Storytellers

Perhaps print media became the early adopters of transmedia storytelling out of necessity. But they certainly were not alone. Most television franchises today are built with ancillary narratives that support the main storyline. Television producers are becoming very adept at leveraging multiple channels to give further access into the worlds of our favorite shows. Whatever the format, we have all come to expect immersive, cross-channel experiences from our favorite TV shows. Just ask any fan of HBO's *Game of Thrones* and they'll share with you an entire web of narrative formats that expand the franchise beyond the episodes that air on the network.

In the Streaming Era, Television is Thriving

Early on, the naysayers predicted the death of broadcast television. Now that some time has passed, we are beginning to see that the forces of convergence are disrupting old distribution structures. But these forces aren't killing off the media themselves. Today, the television industry is alive and well. In fact, many in the industry have proclaimed that we are now in a second "Golden Age of Television." This idea is so pervasive that it's impossible to provide attribution to its originator. That said, journalist Michael Wolff deserves credit for the headline from his book, "Television is the New Television."

Why is television "the new television"? We are experiencing a creative renaissance in television for two key reasons. First, online streaming—whether intended or incidental—led to a whole new form of television consumption known as "binge viewing." And the truth is, it takes a lot of content to satisfy the appetites of people who consume multiple episodes of a series in one sitting. Binge viewing has created a new demand for libraries of content that, otherwise, would remain sitting on the proverbial shelf. Many franchises now have new generations of fans who watch past seasons, and new revenue from distributors who pay for these libraries of content. In addition, binge viewers are willing to cross over and watch live television if they fall in love with a series that is still on the air. The libraries of past seasons serve as a fantastic sampling mechanism for viewers who were late to the party. It's a win for streaming television and a win for live television as well.

Next, one could argue that binge viewing in the streaming

television era has made live television better. If someone is going to make an appointment to watch a show in real time, it better be worthwhile. To attract audiences, live television is evolving into "event" television that is "must-see" in the moment. Event television remains our best hope for attracting mass audiences. And, many advertisers still need to reach mass audiences as part of their overall marketing strategy. The demand from audiences is still there, and the advertising revenue to fund event television will remain as well.

That Doesn't Mean Things Are Easy for Distributors

The idea that streaming television has made live television even better should not be confused with the challenges that streaming TV services are creating for the cable and satellite industries. In search of more cost-effective ways of accessing their favorite TV content, consumers are "cutting the cord." This way, they can avoid having to pay for bundles of content that do not interest them. But don't forget: This is a distribution issue— not a content issue. Audiences love their TV content whether they watch it live or whether they binge multiple episodes at a time.

We will take another look at the struggles facing distributors who make their money by charging for access to someone else's content when we address the Fifth Global Truth: Content Economics.

Marketers Are Having a Much Harder Time

Unfortunately, while the media themselves are embracing the potential of symbiosis, marketers are having a much more difficult time. Not only are marketers still stuck in silos, many are making things worse by fixating on new silos: Paid, Owned, and Earned Media. These relatively new labels have everything to do with marketing finance and absolutely nothing to do with how audiences experience media in the real world.

When investments in paid media are captured as an expense on the balance sheet, marketers tend to isolate each individual paid media decision and ensure that it delivers an immediate return-on-investment. Marketers have become obsessed with attribution. Marketers not only look at the attribution of a single media channel, they even question every purchase within that channel. If a single media exposure doesn't result in immediate behavior, it is deemed a failure. This "immediate return-on-investment" mindset makes it nearly impossible to build truly integrated media plans that capitalize on the symbiosis within and across channels. Instead, attribution models select "winners" and "losers."

When marketers focus on the return-on-investment of every discrete media purchase, it becomes hard to see the big picture. Not only are marketers losing sight of how media work together in symbiosis, they are missing opportunities to deliver transmedia stories that will engage their customers rather than annoy them. We pay lip-service to the potential of transmedia storytelling. Then, instead, we settle for "integrated" ad campaigns that have a "similar look and feel."

From Budgets to "Bait," Marketers Are Missing the Point

Think about how far off course we have drifted: marketers are excited by the idea of changing the design of a digital ad in real time to improve the responsiveness of the ad. But if you change the message to bait the audience into clicking, how does that impact other parts of the brand narrative that are being communicated in other channels? Perhaps we are giving too much credit to digital advertising to begin with. More often, the messaging is direct response in nature as opposed to part of a broader brand narrative. If marketers continue to bait audiences, eventually those audiences will catch on and simply ignore or even block the bait.

Marketers tend to drift even further away from symbiosis when they're threatened with budget cuts. Because media channels have different degrees of financial flexibility associated with them, marketers tend to modify media plans based upon which channel is most flexible, or cancellable. As a result we are often left with "half" conversations that aren't reinforced in other media.

Unfortunately, when marketers are slow to embrace media symbiosis, it limits media companies as well. Any media company that relies primarily upon advertising revenue can embrace symbiosis only as far as those who are paying the bills are willing to think the same way. As long as marketers remain fixated on channels, media companies will be forced to fight the fight one channel at a time as well.

TRUTH

In order to embrace symbiosis, we have to continue to study it and then model its effects so that marketers will have the evidence they need to relax their current hyper-focus on every single paid media expenditure and, instead, focus on the Big Picture. The more empirical evidence we can gather, the easier it will become for marketers to stop building marketing plans one-channel-at-a-time.

Research, Models and Technology Are Ready for Symbiosis

Fortunately, evidence is catching up to insight. Research from Northwestern University's Spiegel Research Center illustrate what they call "The Consumer Engagement Engine." Like gears in an engine that affect other cogs and wheels, any discrete activity at one end of the marketing spectrum can greatly influence another. And, the process is shared between marketers and their customers.

Further, market mix models are starting to change. In addition to modeling the impact of each channel in isolation, marketers can now study "the synergy effect"—the incremental response of coordinated efforts that cannot be explained by any single channel alone. Further, marketing technologies are now helping us put these empirical findings into action. Thanks to new customer journey management technology, marketers can more effectively deliver transmedia stories along the unique pathways of individual consumers in near real time and at scale. The research, the models and the technology are ripe for symbiosis.

Budgets and Marketing Plans Need to Change, Too

Next, we need to change the process marketers use to develop marketing plans, both internally and in collaboration with their external agency partners. In order to build cross-channel conversations with customers, we need to create a process that puts the right people in the room at the right time. All the stakeholders will then have to rally around the same outcome. The marketing team and their external partners will either win as a team, or they will all go down together.

It's not only the way we collaborate that needs to change: we need to reexamine the way we set budgets, too. Specifically, we need to keep budgets as fluid as possible. Instead of assigning them at the beginning of the process, marketers should move budgeting all the way to the end. When budgets are set too early in the process, it reinforces old behavior and limits the potential for symbiosis to occur.

Perhaps this new integrated process will lead to a re-bundling of marketing services. Only time will tell. Regardless, integration is a mindset more than a structure. Marketers who are willing to relax their scrutiny of every single maneuver to focus on what's truly important will win in this new media world.

Reminder: Content Matters

Finally, new market mix models and a new process won't change a thing unless we embrace new marketing content. Content should draw audiences in and then guide them to other channels. This is how transmedia storytelling works. You start a conversation in one medium, and then you deepen it across other media. We have a long way to go. But we are on our way.

CHAPTER SIX

GLOBAL TRUTH #3
CIRCUITS

Circuit (n): the route traveled, a two-way communication path between points, the complete path of an electric current, including usually the source of electric energy.

(Source: Merriam-webster.com)

> *TRUTH: It's human nature to share, and the digital structure of media makes it easy to do. All it takes is a mouse, smartphone, or other digital sharing device to take content from one channel and place it onto another. Consumers are no longer recipients of content. Instead, they're accelerants who move content along open media circuits to reach networks of friends and followers at the "speed of share."*

What do circuits and the basic principles of electric currents have to do with the media? Circuitry is a simple but powerful metaphor to describe how content flows across media channels from sender, to receiver, and back again. Once upon a time, the media circuits (i.e., the pathways by which content flowed from sender to receiver) worked pretty much like a closed circuit. Content flowed from Point A to Point B with limited disruption. And each medium operated on its own circuit. Television content flowed across television circuits. Magazine content traveled along magazine circuits, and so on. The various media circuits ran parallel to each other. There wasn't much mingling.

Consumers Used to Be The Endpoints

Who was responsible for turning on/off the media circuits? Content distribution and flow used to be in the hands of professionals in the media and marketing industries. The consumer was the endpoint of all our efforts. Consumers were the Point Bs, the recipients of what the professional content producers curated for them, and all the advertising that came along with it. In marketing terms, we called this phenomenon "push" marketing.

When media circuits were closed, advertising content could travel only as fast as media channels could accumulate their audiences. We placed messages in specific channels and we waited for a week, four weeks or for entire purchase cycles to accumulate effects. The process was slow, cumbersome and expensive. We had to pay for every opportunity to engage with audiences. To make matters worse, the reach potential of any particular media channel was inherently limited. As we spent more money, our efforts would begin to pile up frequency against the same audience, leading to message wear-out.

Content Doesn't Stay Put Anymore

Someone or something opened the circuits. Content doesn't stay put anymore. It can start on one channel and seamlessly jump onto another. Some call it leaky media. Others call it displacement. Regardless of the label you assign to the phenomenon, the result is the same: it's hard to contain great content. The great stuff will leap across media channels showing up just about everywhere.

How prolific is channel leaping? Just ask one famous

woman: Mona Lisa. If *The Mona Lisa* could do more than "smile," she might share the story from her many travels across media circuits far beyond the Louvre. If someone asked you to name the media channel that delivers *The Mona Lisa* to the world, you would most likely answer, "the Louvre." But that answer is only partially true. If you went to the Louvre, you would see hundreds of visitors standing in front of the iconic image with their digital photo devices held high. All it takes is a simple click—and a matter of seconds—for *The Mona Lisa* to travel across media circuits, her face landing on every social media channel imaginable.

TECHNOLOGY

What caused the circuits to open? Empowered consumers armed with digital photo or video devices. That's it! So long as content can be digitized, it can travel on/off/across nearly every media platform imaginable. Remember, thanks to convergence, most media have some form of digital structure. This makes it easy to open the circuits and move content around at the consumer's whim.

Today, Content Flows as Fast as a Network Connection

This act of movement becomes even more profound when you think about the incredible speeds by which this "channel leaping" occurs. Content can now flow as fast as a network connection—and that's fast! This acceleration of content across open circuits makes old, Newtonian media planning time feel like slow motion. Think about it. We used to count media plan intervals in weekly and four-week purchase cycles. Now we measure content distribution and flow based upon the speed of our connections. It's near instant.

Consumers Now Have a Place to Post Stuff That Interests Them

Finally, all this displaced content needs somewhere to go. Consumers can pull content off channels, but they can't easily put content back onto traditional media channels. That responsibility still lies in the hands of professionals. Enter social media channels. Consumers now have a place to post "stuff" that interests them. And, based upon the size of their networks, this content can reach a whole new audience beyond what was planned and budgeted for.

Consumers Are No Longer Recipients—They're Accelerants

While technology was necessary to open the circuits, technology is only an accomplice to a much bigger phenomenon. We have now fundamentally shifted the role of the consumer in the marketing paradigm. Some may call this the shift from "push" to "pull," but this description doesn't go far enough. Consumers do more than pull content along; thanks to open circuits, they can now accelerate great content experiences. Their impact is truly exponential. This is why we can call the current media era "the Era of Exponential Effects."

What do we mean by acceleration? Think about it. Now consumers can act in real time, influencing hundreds, thousands, or even millions of people in their social networks. Thanks to social media, word of mouth has become exponential. The idea of target audience reach is forever changed. Once we reach consumers, they now hold the power to amplify our efforts based upon the size of their email distribution lists and the number of friends and followers they have on various social media platforms. And those secondary audiences can do the same thing. It goes on and on…exponentially!

Consumers are now the most potent channel we have. Frankly, they always were. But now? Armed with everyday technology, consumers can accelerate great content to vast networks at "The Speed of Share."

PIONEERS

Embracing the true potential of open media circuits requires a willingness to let go and put your fate in the hands of your customer. The indie rock band Oasis understood its fan base so well that it was willing to hand over the launch of its 2008 album, *Dig Out Your Soul*, to the very people that would make its music a hit: the audience. This pioneering case turned every paradigm known to the music industry upside down.

Here's What Happens When You Engage Your Fans

Oasis understood that its fate was no longer tied to the promise of airplay from the once powerful radio disc jockeys. Rather, the band saw that it only became truly successful once its music landed on the streets. So Oasis had the brilliant idea to start at the end. The band handed four tracks from its upcoming album over to noted street musicians in New York City. The idea was: Why not have fans discover the music and share the experience with others?

And share they did! The street music became a groundswell that was shared via mobile media and tracked with geotagging. Oasis captured the entire experience as a documentary film that aired on the band's MySpace page. Ultimately, the mainstream media covered the experience as a story as opposed to the traditional coverage of an album review. As a result, Oasis's "*Dig Out Your Soul*" became the first top ten album the band had in more than 10 years.

What makes this case so special? If you ask the members of Oasis, they'll point to the album's success. But for students of the media, this case demonstrates what can happen when a single piece of compelling content is shared freely by fans. Think about it. A live street performance fueled media experiences across several different media channels: live events, mobile/geotagged media, social media and mainstream media.

Historically, we would have produced very specific pieces of content, and then sent them on their way from Point A to Point B on fixed channels. We would need the songs themselves, music videos, concert tours, ads in music magazines, press interviews and a digital campaign to fulfill the individual requirements of fixed media channels.

Not anymore. Oasis demonstrated that media circuits are wide open and that an engaged consumer will accelerate content across media networks when it "turns them on." Finally, let's give credit where credit is due. The music—both the original music and the interpretations by the street musicians—was damn good and worth sharing!

How can we quantify the Oasis experience? What was the target audience reach and frequency generated by the experience? How many impressions did we accumulate during the purchase cycle? What was the ROI of each medium in the mix? Clearly, these are the wrong questions to ask. Why do we still ask them? Because we're still stuck with those old, Newtonian media measures!

TRAVELING THROUGH CHAOS

The Oasis case was a brilliant demonstration of social media in action. But which medium was the social medium? Therein lies one of the biggest problems plaguing us today: we confuse the terms "social media" and "social platforms."

Marketers Treat Social Media like a Tactic—but It's Really an Outcome

Let's get this straight: social media is not a tactic. It is not a line item on a marketing plan, a specific channel or form of content. Rather, it is an outcome, and no single channel has a lock on the social nature of content. Every single medium is only one click removed from the conduit that enables consumers to take the content and share it. Any medium can serve as the starting point of a journey that can take a great piece of content across open circuits and into vast networks of hearts and minds.

Given the confusion around what is truly "social media," it's no surprise that before we could blink, marketers jumped onto every social platform imaginable with their best guess at the types of branded content that could engage the audiences on these platforms. Then, practically every form of a marketer's outbound communication encouraged consumers to "like" them on Facebook, use their hashtags on Twitter, or follow their YouTube channel or Instagram page. It's as if marketers attempted to build branded barricades on platforms that were meant to be open lanes.

Marketers quickly learned that the brand destinations they built on social platforms required all kinds of support. These destinations didn't magically sustain themselves, nor did hordes of consumers gravitate to them without a good reason to do so. Marketers needed to spend money—and in some instances quite a sizable sum—to produce new forms of content that suited these platforms.

But even with engaging content, many brands became lost in all the clutter that quickly built up on these platforms. And it didn't help matters that some social media platforms changed their algorithms to make it less likely that a brand's content would organically show up on the feeds of its desired customers. This gave birth to a new form of marketing spending, where marketers began paying to promote their own presence on social media platforms. What started as a free and open circuit for all quickly became a cost on the marketer's balance sheet.

Social Media Ads Are Big Business

Paid advertising on social media channels has become big business. In its 2016 year-end earnings report, Facebook reported advertising revenue of $26.8 billion. Nope, that "b" is not a typo! Has Facebook lost its soul? Maybe, but that's a different book for a different day. The reality is: no single media company can sustain itself without revenue. In the words of Shelly Palmer, a respected marketing and technology consultant, "I pay, you pay, or someone else pays." And in the case of most social platforms, their primary source of revenue has become advertising.

Marketers Can't Stop the Flow of Consumer Engagement

Has all this marketing interference destroyed these social platforms? While they have become clogged with billions of dollars' worth of paid advertising, they surprisingly still work as we first imagined. All these distracting ads on social platforms are nothing more than inconvenient speed bumps along what remains a superhighway for consumers to accelerate content that touches them. This serves as further proof that consumers are, indeed, the most valuable media channel in the mix. Even when marketers attempt to intervene, they can no longer stop the flow of consumer engagement. The best thing that marketers can do is learn to share the process with consumers. Otherwise, they will be left behind.

As we learned from the Oasis case, this new relationship between marketers and consumers can become a "win/win." The band had the humility and the restraint to cede control of their own album launch, putting their fate into the hands of their fans. However, this relationship cannot be forced or bought. Rather, consumer involvement is a privilege that must be earned.

"Paid Influencer Marketing" Could Destroy
"Word of Mouth"

Unfortunately, some marketers are trying to game the system by paying for influence rather than earning it organically. Welcome to the era of "paid influencer marketing." According to reports by CBS news, this category of advertising has quickly grown into a billion-dollar industry. Paid influencer marketing creates a financial incentive for Key Opinion Leaders (KOLs) to spread a marketer's message among their networks of friends, fans and followers. A KOL can be anyone from a celebrity, to a teenage blogger who blossomed into a YouTube sensation, to someone who is considered an expert in a particular field.

Paid promotions are nothing new, and at face value they are just another form of advertising. However, they become problematic when these endorsements are not properly labeled as "sponsored." Unfortunately, too many amateur spokespeople do not comply with FTC guidelines for labeling the sponsored content on their social media channels as #sponsored, #ad, or #partner. Luckily, the FTC is taking notice. In the spring of 2017 they issued 90 warning letters to well-known celebrities who were not complying with labeling guidelines for sponsored posts.

Those 90 celebrities are just the tip of the iceberg. The deceptive labeling issue is rampant and hard to regulate given the size and scope of the influencer ecosystem. It is going to take tougher consumer protection laws and significantly more resources to enforce compliance. For now, we are left with a deluge of deceptive "word of mouth" recommendations. These recommendations are grossly misleading and could actually damage the effects of "consumers as accelerants." If consumers no longer believe the intentions behind someone sharing a marketer's message, we will destroy the gift of word of mouth.

Remember: Consumer Engagement Is a Privilege That Must Be Earned

Perhaps the greatest lesson learned as marketers fumble their way through these open media circuits is one of humility. Marketers can't control consumer behavior. They can't force it by opening up their wallets. And there are no clear-cut rules for creating social experiences that can organically travel across open circuits. If any so-called experts claim to know the answers, don't believe them. There is no such thing as "viral marketing." Going "viral" is a privilege that must be earned as opposed to a tactic that can be deployed.

TRUTH

Brace Yourself for the Wild West of Media Planning

If content can travel freely across open media circuits and marketers must now share the process with consumers, does it make sense to attempt to build media plans anymore? Indeed, we have entered a Wild West of media planning. But that doesn't mean we should throw the media plan out the window. Rather, we need to accept that media planning is much more relative than it used to be. And that's a good thing! Marketers and media strategists should start off with a solid blueprint that is informed by customer journeys and big, creative ideas. Then, if all goes well, we can delight in seeing that blueprint shift and grow as consumers add dimension to the scope and structure of our plans.

Here's How the Media Planning Process Needs to Change

For starters, we must change the way we identify and value the right audience for a marketer's message. In the past, we studied the demographic characteristics of current and potential users of product categories and specific brands to arrive at a "target audience" for media plans. It's time to retire the term "target audience." Consumers are not "targets." A target is something you aim at—and shoot things at.

Consumers are far more important than the term "target audience" suggests. If we engage them, they will become the most valuable media channel in the mix by spreading messages far beyond the reach and scope of any paid media plan. An engaged consumer doesn't care about whether they are in a marketer's intended "target" audience. And they will share high quality content across their networks—regardless of how well their networks fit the defined characteristics of a marketer's customer profile. And if someone outside of the marketer's definition of a customer becomes inspired, all the better!

Next, we must reconsider how we determine which media channels are most effective for reaching and engaging audiences. Unfortunately, media channels tend to get credit based upon their ability to "reach" an audience. But that is only the very first step in a much more dynamic phenomenon: an engaged audience seizing on great content and sending it along a new circuit. The media mix models need to catch up to this wonderful phenomenon and better capture how content leaps effortlessly off one channel and onto another. Which channel gets credit for consumer engagement: the originating channel or the "jump" channel? The answer should be "all of the above."

Further, we must acknowledge that the traditional measures of media plan reach and frequency are far too simple for what is truly happening today. Measuring the "opportunity to see" a marketer's message based upon the paid media schedule is only the first step. It in no way truly reflects the actual reach of the plan. The true reach of our efforts will be exponential thanks to the scope of each engaged consumer's network. We're better off saving the counting for the end!

Finally, you can launch great content in practically any medium. If it's truly worth sharing, it will travel at an incredible speed among well-established networks of hearts and minds. But remember, content won't land anywhere—let alone everywhere—if it isn't worth sharing in the first place. We need to refocus our efforts toward the creative product itself. Spoken from a true media professional, "Content was, is, and will remain king!"

CHAPTER SEVEN

GLOBAL TRUTH #4 BRANDS

Brand (n): a class of goods identified by name as the product of a single firm or manufacturer.

(Source: Merriam-webster.com)

> **TRUTH: Media were once defined by their distribution technology. Today, media have to distinguish themselves in ways that go beyond function and form. They need to become transmedia brands that are built upon promises delivered across any platform imaginable: today, tomorrow and into the future. Media distribution may be transient, but transmedia brands can stand the test of time and channel.**

What do the media have in common with the idea of branding? Unfortunately, not much…yet! The media have long operated under a functional model that is based upon two foundational variables:

Distribution: This is the definition of the term "medium" in the first place. It's the idea that a medium represents a unique distribution pathway that enables content to flow from its source to an audience.

Audience: The number of individuals who show up

on a channel. Their attention can then be sold to marketers who wish to advertise their products and services to them.

In the Past, the Media Didn't Need to Become Brands

Once upon a time and not too long ago, this functional model seemed to work. Historically, media distribution pathways were relatively fixed and a bit more proprietary. The technology was not particularly friendly to redundancy. There was only so much room on the broadcast spectrum. There were only so many poles and lines that could run down a street. And a print distribution network was costly and complicated to build.

In addition, once audiences selected their medium of choice, they tended to spend the bulk of their time with said medium—usually to the exclusion of others. Media consumption analyses used to illustrate the "seesaw effect." If you were a heavy user of one medium, you tended to be a light to non-user of another.

There was no need for the media to become brands because branding only becomes important when product function is no longer enough. Brands take what are otherwise redundant products or services and make them special. Brands live beyond function; rather, they provide promises that create emotional bonds between the brand and the consumer.

Well, the time has come. The old model is broken. Any media enterprise that defines its strategy solely by its means of distribution will likely fail. There is nothing proprietary or particularly compelling about distribution pathways. The media themselves are becoming a commodity.

TECHNOLOGY

The same technology story that is underlying the forces of media convergence is coming into play once again. Distribution pathways are no longer proprietary. Once media content is digitized, it loses the safety of a distribution silo that is suited for a very specific format: broadcast, newsprint, glossy paper, cable conduit, etc. Even what was once proprietary to a computer screen or mobile device faces the same competition from a host of legacy media that have now migrated into the digital media space. All digital content travels along the same digital highway.

Just a few short years ago, when *Media: From Chaos to Clarity* was first published, the primary distribution channel for each medium still offered a sense of protection and identity. We could envision a future that would be governed by the forces of media convergence, but it wasn't yet a reality. We talked about the need for branding that would transcend channels but the need didn't seem critical. We thought we had more time to figure it all out.

Today, Media Enterprises Have to Compete Across Multiple Channels

We were wrong! Audiences seamlessly travel between "legacy" channels and digital channels. Digital adoption advanced unlike any rate of media adoption that we had seen before. Today, most media enterprises compete across multiple channels and they are faced with a host of competition for the time and attention of audiences unlike anything they have ever experienced.

To complicate matters further, digital distribution is relatively inexpensive and readily available to anyone who wishes to enter the media business. All it takes is 10 dollars to register a domain name and download some basic software such as WordPress, and anyone and everyone can enter the media business. Professional media companies, marketers and even consumers themselves are now bumping into each other with their own versions of "media" that clog the digital super highways. We have more media than we know what to do with!

If technology has rendered any single medium redundant, what's left for the media to do? It's time to take a lesson from every other category that deals with redundant products and services. The media must become brands.

The commoditization of media will open up opportunities for those who understand classic brand management and can apply these principles to the media business. That's because media brands must live by the same rules as any other brand.

Every Media Brand Must Have a Promise

Call it what you like: brand essence, brand promise, brand identity, etc. Every media brand must have a soul—a purpose or promise that defines the relationship between the content it delivers and the experience its audience expects. This promise should be able to carry the brand beyond the boundaries of any particular media channel that exists today, tomorrow, or in the future. That is what we mean when we refer to a "transmedia brand:" a brand that can truly transcend the unstable nature of media channels. The future rests with these brands.

PIONEERS

One media brand comes to mind as a true pioneer. This brand took what was otherwise a media commodity and made it special. Not only did it offer a provocative distribution platform, it understood that its distribution platform wasn't the story. Instead, this brand relied on its experience and promise to its audience to carry it forward, through decades and numerous media platforms. This brand is ESPN.

ESPN Makes Serving Sports Fans Its Mission

When ESPN first entered the picture back in 1979, the idea of a cable network that was fully dedicated to sports was quite provocative. But ESPN understood that cable distribution was not the story. At the time, sports coverage was fairly accessible. In any market, you could find sports on pretty much any distribution channel: television, radio, newspaper etc. But ESPN was a bit different. It built a brand on the idea that it would not simply distribute sports content over a cable conduit; rather, it would serve sports fans.

ESPN's mission reads as follows: "To serve sports fans wherever sports are watched, listened to, discussed, debated, read about or played." This notion of service to the fan shapes everything that ESPN does. It infuses a unique personality into the brand's content, and enables ESPN to meet sports fans where they are. Cable network? Yes. Multiple cable networks, in fact. Radio network? Sure! Magazine? Consider it done. Restaurants at Disney theme parks? Absolutely! Web and mobile properties? Of course! So long as ESPN delivers its unique promise to sports fans, the brand can travel well beyond the boundaries of any particular channel.

Despite Cord-Cutting, ESPN's Future Remains Bright

That doesn't mean it's been easy for ESPN. Recently, cable cord-cutting has posed a serious threat to the brand. In 2017, shares of ESPN's parent company, Disney, took a hit. A few months later, the brand underwent a series of highly publicized layoffs. Some questioned whether ESPN could survive the losses in cable carriage fees that, historically, made up half of the brand's revenue.

Without question, falling cable distribution dealt a blow to ESPN's balance sheet. But while a weaker brand would have collapsed under the weight of such adversity, ESPN was able to take the hit. And many signs are pointing to a brighter future for the brand.

Is this view of what's in store for ESPN overly optimistic? Not according to *Forbes*. Back in September 2007, *Forbes* released a valuation of the top sports brands. ESPN took the top spot among sports businesses with a brand value of $7.5 billion. Fast forward ten years to 2017 and, despite all the uncertainty in the cable television industry, ESPN's brand value, as reported by *Forbes*, has skyrocketed to $15.8 billion.

TRAVELING THROUGH CHAOS

Unfortunately, we can count the number of true transmedia brands in existence today on one hand (OK, maybe two hands). That's a big problem! There are a host of reasons why this is the case and we can blame all sides of the industry: the media themselves, advertisers and even audiences.

Building a Transmedia Brand Is Hard—Just Look at MTV

Some media companies are run by management teams who cannot see beyond their original channel. Such is the case with Viacom and its once crown jewel, MTV. The acronym MTV stands for "Music Television." This was a truly revolutionary concept back in August 1981, when MTV signed on the air with its infamous "Video Killed the Radio Star" music video.

After its launch, MTV quickly became the media

brand of a generation. Those of us who witnessed this phenomenon first hand were labeled "The MTV Generation." That was then. This is now. Over time, music migrated from television screens to digital screens. But MTV didn't follow suit. Its owner, Viacom, saw MTV first and foremost as a cable television network. It ceded the migration of music onto digital platforms to the likes of Sony and Apple, opting to revamp its cable network schedule with reality TV fare. Remember "Jersey Shore?" Hopefully, you don't!

Instead of adapting to new mediums, MTV chose to compete as a cable television network geared toward young adults. Unfortunately, this demographic was quickly migrating onto other media formats, leaving the world of cable television far behind. Today, the MTV Generation is long gone and the brand is a mere shadow of its former self. In fact, as of 2017, MTV has fallen off brand consultancy Interbrand's ranking of the Top 100 Global Brands.

Branding Matters for New Media, Too

The fall of MTV isn't only a lesson for legacy media. New and emerging media will realize the same fate if they cannot quickly transition from being a "technology darling" to a true transmedia brand. New technologies can only hold the interest of their audiences and the industry at large for so long. If they don't evolve into brands that offer permanence and promise in their audiences' lives, these darlings will meet the same fate as the old-guard media that refused to adapt.

If you need proof, just consider all the startups that were once darlings of the media industry and are now either shadows of their former selves or out of business entirely. Remember MySpace? The platform was truly revolutionary, but it was displaced by Facebook. Why? Because being among the first social platforms simply wasn't good enough when a better alternative came along. And remember when Vine videos were all the rage? Vine's no longer in business. Its most recent owner, Twitter, shut the site down at the beginning of 2017. Will Snapchat make it? Time will tell, but this author is a skeptic.

The landscape is littered with technology companies that didn't move beyond their functional product offering toward something more permanent and meaningful in their customers' lives. As a result, the media industry is filled with once shiny objects that are now nothing more than discarded litter alongside the vast super highway.

Advertising Budgets Are Slowing Progress

Why are some media companies unwilling to let go of their legacies? Just follow the money. An advertiser-supported media company can shift its mindset only to the degree that advertisers are willing to follow suit. If advertisers are stuck in the past, it's hard for media companies to move ahead of them. There's simply too much revenue at stake.

Unfortunately, marketers tend to allocate advertising budgets by channel —the very thing that is now redundant and unstable. That means advertising budgets are oftentimes stuck in silos, making it difficult to take advantage of transmedia brand experiences as a result. Let's revisit ESPN. In order to execute a "cross-channel" presence on ESPN, marketers who still set budgets by individual channel will have to tap into television budgets, digital budgets, (both digital display and online video), radio budgets, magazine budgets, mobile budgets and possibly event budgets. It's an accounting nightmare!

Brands Deserve Credit for the Environment they Offer

And with those budgets, what are we purchasing? Media buyers and sellers still fixate on audience impressions. Today, in a world of hyper media consumption, it is rare for any particular medium to attract a truly unduplicated audience that cannot be found elsewhere. Ask any media buyer, and they'll agree that no single media property is a must-buy anymore. A buyer can "buy around" any property and still reach the audience they desire. Until we prove that the environment offered by one media brand makes an advertiser's message more impactful than the environment offered by another, media companies won't get the credit they deserve for curating special experiences that are revered by audiences.

Media Companies Adopt Short-Term Tactics to Appease Advertisers

To make matters worse, advertisers tend to value a particular medium only for the audience it attracts at the exact moment in time when they want to place their message. As a result, media companies often resort to short-term tactics to ensure that the measured audience at any given moment in time meets the advertiser's expectations. When audience expectations fall short, it costs the media company money.

As a result, media companies cannot afford to invest in branding initiatives that can't immediately be monetized. In other industries, companies are rewarded for the loyalty and lifetime value of its customers. In the media business, audiences are only as valuable as their worth to advertisers in the moment. And, that battle is fought 24/7/365.

Audience Loyalty Is Earned in Micro-Moments

Finally, when your product is content, you have to prove your worth to the audience with every show, every post, and every issue. Audience loyalty is earned in micro-moments. It's a tough proposition, but companies that make a clear promise and consistently deliver exemplary content to fulfill that promise will earn the trust and loyalty of audiences.

TRUTH

In a world where most media are sharing the same digital superhighway, and no medium can claim sole ownership of its audience, there's only one way to survive: create a powerful media brand that can move with the marketplace while remaining true to its promise. This should be the top priority for any "medium" in existence today—old or new. In fact, it's a mandate for survival in media chaos.

Building a Transmedia Brand Is Paramount—But It's Not for the Faint of Heart

Remember, anyone can now enter the media business. But few can consistently deliver content that is worth the time and attention of audiences across any channel that is relevant to them. In the few years since *Media: From Chaos to Clarity* was first published, many marketers have started including their own "media-style" communications on their owned media channels. They've been met with mixed results.

Marketers are quickly realizing that the media business isn't for the faint of heart. It's a full-time job to deliver content that serves the wants, needs and interests of the audience. Some marketers can become legitimate transmedia brands themselves because their core business naturally generates content that is of great interest to audiences.

In other instances, the marketer's owned media channel simply becomes advertising that is packaged differently. In order for marketers to compete in this space, they need to think like a media company and put their own vested interests to the side. It may be right for some, but for most marketers entering the media business is not the easiest route to customer engagement.

Over time, marketers will come to understand the true value of media companies that consistently deliver exemplary content across channels. These companies do a much better job of aggregating audiences than most marketers can. And while from a marketing finance standpoint a brand's "owned" media may appear to be "free" exposure, the reality is there are many hidden costs to promoting and maintaining these channels. In many cases, paid advertising on an established media brand will deliver a better return on investment than a commitment to owned channels that don't do a very good job of engaging the audience.

Remember: The Audience Is Your True Customer

In order for media companies to thrive as transmedia brands, they must follow a critical rule of Brand Management: remain relentlessly focused on the customer. Do this, and financial success will follow. Unfortunately, many advertiser-supported media brands are confused about who the customer is. Too often, media companies cater to the whims of advertisers because they are the ones who are paying the bills. This is a dangerous strategy.

In reality, the true customer is not the advertiser. It's the audience. Without them, there is no advertiser. Media companies should focus first and foremost on the audience experience and ensure that advertising models foster engagement. We have a long way to go from current models, which are perceived as intrusive interruptions and in some cases even stalking! But with the right mindset, we can fix these models and make advertising part of an engaging brand experience.

A Transmedia Brand Needs Transmedia Accounting

Finally, transmedia brands call for transmedia accounting practices. Budgetary line items that force big ideas into silos must give way to more holistic accounting. This is a problem on all sides. The media need to do a better job of selling one thing. Media buyers need to do a better job of evaluating one thing. And marketers need to do a better job of funding one thing.

CHAPTER EIGHT

GLOBAL TRUTH #5
ECONOMICS

Economics (n): a social science concerned chiefly with description and analysis of the production, distribution and consumption of goods and services.

(Source: Merriam-webster.com)

> **TRUTH: When media distribution was relatively fixed and limited, media companies could charge audiences for access to their channels. But with increased supply, audiences are trying to pay as little as possible for access. Faced with an abundance of choice, audiences will gravitate toward media that offer the best content experience. And the money soon follows.**

Nothing is Sustainable That's Given Away For Free

In the end, it all comes down to money. The media business is a for-profit enterprise. Nothing is sustainable that is given away for free. But, in media chaos, we're not so sure what part of the media model should make the money and what part (if any) should be free.

At the same time, marketers mandate (and deserve) value from their media investments. But what should they be valuing?

The delivery mechanism itself? The audience? The content? The advertising environment? All of the above? None of the above?

Where Is the Value in the Media Economy?

And while we're asking questions: Where is all the value in the media economy? When new technologies become the darlings of Wall Street and legacy media giants struggle to stay afloat, one has to wonder.

Why are we witnessing such strange valuations in the media economy? Do the basic laws of supply and demand still apply to the media business? According to supply and demand, if you could offer a product or service that was in limited supply yet in high demand, you would make money. Conversely, if you had excess supply on your hands and not enough demand for it, prices would tumble. This seems so logical. So what's going on to explain the economic drivers of the media? That's the key question we will set out to address in this chapter.

TECHNOLOGY

Before the dawn of the digital media era, media distribution pathways used to be in relatively limited supply. It was extremely costly and often times technically prohibitive to support an abundance of platforms. Broadcast media were limited by the bandwidth of the spectrum. And print media were limited by the costs of production (paper/ink/postage) and the costs of distribution (subscriptions and newsstands).

In this paradigm, it made sense that valuation was focused on media distribution systems. The media were in limited supply. Audiences didn't have much choice in the matter. They simply opted in to what was available to them. And the media accommodated them by programming high quality content that had mass appeal. In essence, we were operating in what we called a mass media economy.

Back then, there was only so much room for content. The media providers had to be much more selective in their choice of which content would see the light of day and which content would land on the cutting room floor. As a result, there was a lot of high quality content that didn't make it on the air or in print. The supply of content exceeded the media's capacity to place it all.

Digital Flipped the Supply and Demand Curve

Once media became digitized, the supply equation forever changed. Suddenly, media capacity was no longer an issue. Price of entry was no longer daunting. Capacity was nearly unlimited and far exceeded our ability to fill all the bandwidth. Now? Media supply far exceeds actual demand. We have more digital media pipeline than we can fill.

What happens to the content supply equation when media capacity expands exponentially? All of a sudden, there is a lot more room for a lot more content. And, while anyone can now become a content creator, not everyone can produce high quality content that can attract a large audience. High quality content is now the attractor. And the demand for high quality content now exceeds the supply of it.

In the digital age, media supply is overly abundant. So the value of the pipelines themselves should decline (in theory). Where should we turn our attention instead? Again, content is key. If you follow the laws of supply and demand, high quality content experiences will drive value in the economics of media chaos.

PIONEERS

In order to understand the pioneers in content economics, it's helpful to understand how media typically make money. Media companies have a choice. Remember the words of technology consultant Shelly Palmer? "I pay, you pay, or someone else pays."

Who Pays in the Digital Media World?

Who are the "I," "you" and "someone else" in Shelly Palmer's quote? The "I" are consumers just like you and me. In some instances, audiences will pay a subscription fee or a micro-transaction (also known as a single copy fee) to purchase access to a specific media brand's content. The "you" are advertisers who pay media companies for access to time and space on their platforms so that they can efficiently deliver messages to audiences that gather there. And "someone else" is yet another group: distributors who pay for content, create bundles of it, and then sell it back to audiences (think cable operators and online streaming services).

Over the decades, a pattern emerged: when media content was delivered on the electromagnetic spectrum (such as broadcast television and radio), it was mainly free to audiences and advertiser supported. When media content was delivered on paper—either newsprint or magazine stock—the audience tended to pay for it along with advertisers. And, when media content was delivered through a cable conduit or satellite signal, it was usually bundled with other networks and then offered for a bulk subscription price to audiences. Some of the networks were supported by advertising, while other networks, known as premium networks, were advertising-free.

Advertisers Weren't Willing to Invest in Digital Media

As media content migrated to the internet, the economic model looked very similar to other media that was delivered on the electromagnetic spectrum: it was mainly offered free to audiences. Unlike broadcast television and radio, however, advertisers weren't willing to invest in digital media. The only way that media companies could convince them to invest in digital advertising was by either giving it away as "added value" for advertising investments on legacy platforms, or through a direct-response pricing model where advertisers only paid when someone actually clicked on an ad.

In direct-response, only a fraction of the total audience actually generates monetary value. This generated only pennies on the dollar, leading to media executive Jeff Zucker's infamous quote: "Trading analog dollars for digital pennies." Thus, a tenuous revenue model for an entire sector of the media industry was born. Suddenly, audiences weren't paying and advertisers weren't making up the difference.

High Quality Content Can Fix Poor Economics in Digital Media

Despite this bleak picture, some noteworthy pioneers overcame these unfavorable conditions by building economic models that generated value from the quality of the content itself. These pioneers came from every corner of the media industry, from music, to newspapers to television. Each set bold examples for how content can generate value in this new digital landscape. And we learned something unique from each pioneer.

Radiohead Fans Pick a Price

Back in 2007, online piracy, particularly in music, was soaring. Audiences were taking licensed content without paying a fair price. Often, they wouldn't pay anything at all. Since the digital firewalls were permeable anyway, the British band Radiohead decided to open the gates. The band had just ended their contract with their record label. So they had the freedom to distribute their seventh studio album, *In Rainbows*," directly on their website. The band left it up to each individual fan to decide the price they were willing to pay to download the album.

Not surprisingly, 60 percent of downloads went free of charge. But the other 40 percent commanded an average price of $8.05 per download, according to comScore. The fans set the demand curve, and the content experience paid it off. The album received rave critical reviews. In the end, fans bought 1.75 million *In Rainbows* CDs, according to *Wired*. Clearly, the music was great and worth paying for! The release of "In Rainbows" taught us that customers can be trusted to set pricing. If there's value for them, then they're willing to pay.

The Wall Street Journal Builds a Paywall

Back in the early days of digital media, most newspapers made the mistake of putting all their content online for free. But as audiences migrated onto digital platforms, they soon realized that the stories they were paying for in newsprint were available for free on the paper's website.

This was a double hit to newspaper economics: print subscriptions began to decline, and as circulation numbers dropped, advertising revenue declined as well. Unfortunately, newspapers' digital ad revenue could not even begin to fill the revenue gap caused by declines in print circulation and ad revenue. For these reasons, many newspapers are still financially unsustainable to this day.

But *The Wall Street Journal* chose a different path. Back in 1997, well before audiences had migrated onto digital media in droves, the *WSJ* implemented a "paywall." If people wanted to access the paper's online content, they had to pay to get past a digital firewall.

Why was *The Wall Street Journal* able to do this? They believed in the quality and singularity of their content product. Despite the fact that other newspapers were creating a glut of free news content online, the *WSJ* believed that their world-class financial news content was specialized enough—and high quality enough—that it would still be in demand. Because this content still remained relatively scarce, *The Wall Street Journal* could charge an access fee that their audience was willing to pay.

Hulu Provides Content Worth Paying For

As we learned earlier, when Hulu launched back in 2007, others laughed at the venture—literally! Hulu was nicknamed "Clown Co" by naysayers who thought everything about Hulu—its ownership, its management team, its corporate culture and its premise—was a recipe for failure. The brainchild of two broadcast competitors, NBC and Fox, Hulu represented a radical departure from business as usual right from the outset. Since when do two competitors collaborate to shape their destiny?

Unlike other networks, NBC and FOX realized that if they didn't create an online destination for their television content, it would continue to be shared illegally across open digital media circuits. They had two choices. They could try to shut down piracy and sue the offenders—the pathway that Viacom choose back in 2007 when it sued YouTube for copyright infringement. Or, they could create a place online for all this high quality television content to live, where broadcast networks could earn the revenue they deserved. The second choice is what Hulu's is all about. Hulu was the first online portal built specifically for television content.

Hulu's original finance model mirrored that of other broadcast models. It was offered free to audiences and it relied solely on advertiser support to sustain itself. The founders understood that advertisers need high quality content as much as audiences do. They certainly weren't guaranteed a safe content environment on YouTube (frankly, they still aren't today). So until the content that advertisers knew and trusted migrated onto digital channels, all that television advertising revenue was bound to remain stuck in the television silo.

Hulu's Quality Content Breaks the
"Digital Pennies" Paradigm

Perhaps Hulu deserves more credit than it has received from media analysts and historians. True, the early days of Hulu were quite tenuous. Its first CEO, Jason Kilar, left the company in frustration. And for a period of time, the networks were even looking to sell the company. However, Hulu worked through these challenges, ultimately demonstrating that high quality video content could break the "digital pennies" paradigm. Fast forward just ten short years: Hulu's projected year-end revenues for 2017 are $2.4 billion. Not bad for a company nicknamed "Clown Co," that's for sure!

This revenue figure holds an even more important insight: only 40 percent of that revenue is expected to come from advertisers. The other 60 percent is coming from audience subscriptions. Hulu demonstrated that broadcast media did not always need to be free. Instead of relying totally on advertisers for revenue, Hulu launched a series of subscription tiers. Audiences could pay a lower subscription fee and still receive advertising. Or, if they chose, they could pay a higher subscription fee for an ad-free experience.

Today, Hulu content is no longer available for free. And that's a good thing! Premium content commands value. When something is free, we question its value. Or even worse, we question its motives. We'll explore this in greater detail as we travel through chaos.

TRAVELING THROUGH CHAOS

It didn't take long for many in the industry to catch on to the idea that content is the real driver of value in today's media economy. But this knowledge doesn't make the journey through chaos any easier. Content economics has its own set of consequences that create winners and losers in the media economy. As we travel through chaos, we are going to need to add new terms to our vocabulary in order to understand the power of content: windowing, bundling and clickbait.

Great Content Is Still Scarce

Why is great content so lucrative? First, it's relatively scarce. Content development is still a highly creative endeavor, which means that truly breakthrough content requires resources and skills that very few possess. In addition, it's quite "hit or miss." For every breakthrough piece of content in any medium, there is a glut of mediocre content as well. That means content creators have to cover their costs by generating a high return from a very small percentage of their portfolio.

Luckily, content isn't used up when it's consumed. Content creators can sell and resell their content to the highest bidders. This is known as "content licensing and syndication." And remember all that excess capacity we now have thanks to an explosion of digital media pathways? Because the supply and demand equation has flipped, content producers are finding that suitors will enter into bidding wars to secure the rights to distribute great content on their platforms.

So How Do Distributors Keep Great Content
Locked Up? Windowing

What happens when a particular media distributor wins a bidding war for great content? The people who pay big money to outbid the competition have a vested interest in keeping that great content locked up on their circuits. If content is exclusively available at one destination, the audience will flow to that destination and the media distributor can earn back their investment through audience subscriptions, advertiser revenue or both. This practice of making content available exclusively through a single media distributor for a specific period of time is called "windowing." Once the window of time and place expires, the content producer can resell the same content to another distributor, and so on.

The practice of "windowing" creates firewalls and silos in a media world that, otherwise, would be much more open thanks to the forces of convergence and circuits. It further demonstrates that this new media world revolves around content. Without it, media distributors are nothing more than empty pipelines.

This helps to explain why many content distributors have entered the content production business themselves. If a content distributor produces its own high quality content, it can avoid the bidding wars and earn a greater return on its investment. And once a distributor reaps all the benefits from the content on its own channels, it can then license the content to someone else. Thus, the process of "windowing" continues on.

Well-Curated Bundles Keep Audiences Coming Back For More

When audiences show up on a media distributor's

channel to consume a noteworthy piece of content, it's the job of the media distributor to keep them there. So how can media distributors build audience loyalty? First and foremost, they must offer a seamless delivery experience that crosses any and all screens imaginable at a reasonable price. But frankly, this is only a price of entry. Convenient access at an affordable price will not sustain a media enterprise by itself. Instead, it is incumbent upon the media distributor to curate a bundled content experience that the audience will want to stick around for.

A content curator takes the guesswork out of the equation by sorting through all the available content and selecting what is truly worth the time and attention of the audience. He or she then packages that content into convenient bundles. These content bundles take on many forms: a selection of relevant cable networks, a library of streaming video content, a magazine issue, a news website, or perhaps a playlist of songs.

Regardless of form, all curated bundles share a common thread: an editorial point of view. Bundles lend context and perspective to help the audience choose one experience over another. And when individual pieces of content are bundled together, it creates a more seamless experience for the user and saves them the time it would take to hunt for great content themselves.

So Do Audiences like Bundles or Not?

Content bundles play a critical role in the media landscape. Unfortunately, we have the narrative wrong. Recent consumer backlash against the high price of media has been misinterpreted as a rebellion against bundles. Is this truly the case? Or are audiences rebelling against something else—like the high fees charged for some content bundles?

As we learned earlier, the cable and satellite television

distribution industry has been hit hard by "cord cutting" in recent years. Many consumers are cancelling their cable and/or satellite subscriptions in favor of less expensive options for accessing television content. In response, many cable and satellite providers are offering "skinnier" bundles of content at a lower price.

Perhaps they're offering up the wrong solution. It isn't the bundle that's being rejected; rather, it's the price charged for the bundle that's gotten out of hand. When cord cutters abandon their cable or satellite subscriptions, they oftentimes subscribe to more reasonably priced bundled content services such as Hulu or Netflix rather than pure à la carte or "skinnier" bundled options.

There is evidence across all corners of the media industry that audiences prefer content bundles over à la carte options. Nearly every media sector has content hubs that offer their audience access to a large selection of curated content. Music streaming services such as Spotify provide unlimited access to thousands of curated channels based upon the subscriber's listening preferences—all for one low subscription price. Magazines are still curated into issues that contain multiple articles on a central editorial theme, and newspapers articles are still organized into feature sections. The whole is still greater than the sum of the parts.

If there is so much evidence in support of content bundles, why are we getting the narrative wrong? Perhaps we are confusing the real issue, price elasticity, with the separate issue of whether content should remain bundled or à la carte. It's important that we do not accidentally advocate for an unbundled media world just to contain costs. An unbundled world would have dire consequences for all parties involved. Just study the role of hubs in network science and you'll understand why.

Audiences Are Actually Rejecting Bloated Bundles

Unfortunately, content hubs can be expensive to curate. This links back to the content bidding wars described above. Oftentimes, a content creator will package their own bundle of less desirable content along with their most desirable fare and present the opportunity as "all or nothing" to the bidder. This forces the distributor to take on content that is not necessarily desired by the audience. When the content bundle becomes bloated like this, ultimately, the cost for less desirable fare is passed along to the consumer. It creates a perfect storm.

Even media companies who produce and distribute their own content tend to bloat their channels with less desirable content. Given that digital capacity is nearly insatiable, there is now real estate for content that used to land on the cutting room floor and not see the light of day in the analog media world. While this content doesn't appear in prime positions, it offers the potential to attract "some" audience that can then be monetized with advertising revenue.

In order to preserve the integrity of content bundles, we need to eliminate the dead weight from the bundle. If content isn't worth the audience's time and attention, it shouldn't be included. This is the best way of creating a "skinny bundle" that benefits everyone. Unfortunately, this is easier said than done. That's because in an advertiser-supported media economy, all forms of content have the potential to earn revenue—not just the highest quality fare. If someone shows up to consume the content and that someone fits the criteria that an advertiser is looking for, the advertiser will still invest in delivering an ad in that particular media occurrence. Perhaps the price paid isn't nearly as high as the price paid for premium content. Nonetheless, it's still revenue that goes to the bottom line and subsidizes the cost of the bundle for both the audience and the distributor.

Clickbait Is a Dangerous Scheme

Speaking of revenue from less than desirable content, a new form of content known as "clickbait" is polluting our media circuits. What is clickbait? Basically, it's content that is produced for the sole purpose of getting the audience to "click" on it so that an ad can be served. Clickbait is oftentimes syndicated by companies whose intention is to earn advertising revenue from audience members who fall for the bait. Have you ever encountered a content blurb that claims a celebrity has died? Most of us simply can't help ourselves! Then, when a host of digital ads takes over our screens, we chastise ourselves for falling prey to the scheme.

Consumer protections against clickbait are not yet on the books. Hopefully, by the time the third edition of this book is published, things will have changed. But right now, the only safeguard against clickbait rests with each publisher who allows the practice to occur on their channel in the first place. Relatively recently, Facebook announced that any content with clickbait characteristics will be penalized in its algorithms. But we need to go further and wipe out this practice altogether.

Perhaps the power lies with consumers. If we show our disdain by boycotting advertisers who serve messages adjacent to clickbait and leaving specific channels that still make the time and space for the practice, this irritating phenomenon may finally disappear.

TRUTH

The fifth global truth—that content is the real value driver of the media economy—is the last in order for an important reason: it will be the most difficult truth to realize. That's because for any media company that relies on advertising, content is a means to an end.

To understand why, let's revisit Professor Philip Napoli's book *Audience Economics,* which explains it best. Napoli says that the media produce and distribute content in order to attract audiences that are of interest and value to advertisers. Advertisers rent access to these audiences by purchasing time and space from a media company. Napoli refers to this as the "dual product marketplace." The content product that is distributed by the media company attracts an audience product of particular size and value to advertisers.

Marketers Bid One Cookie at a Time

Why is this such an important distinction? Prior to advances in programmatic buying methods, the content product and the audience product were inextricably linked. You could not buy access to the audience product without first making the decision to purchase advertising adjacent to a particular piece of content. Advertising messages would then reach 100 percent of the audience that was consuming a particular piece of content— whether all of the audience was of value to the advertiser or not.

Today, programmatic buying enables marketers to bid on audiences "one cookie at a time." Advertisers no longer need to buy the content product and accept 100 percent of the audience that comes along with it. Rather, they can set their sights on individual cookies and follow that cookie wherever it lands in the digital media ecosystem. If it's more cost effective to bid on the cookie in one media environment over another, the programmatic model will reward that opportunity.

Where does this leave media companies who invest large sums of money in a high quality content product? They only earn the going market rate for the value of the audience that lands on their content. So you can see why over-investing in content relative to the value return on the audience becomes problematic.

But Some Media Companies Aren't Having It

Media companies are fighting back by creating private marketplaces and inviting advertisers who appreciate the value of the surrounding content to participate. Should a publisher who invests great sums of money in their content product have to compete with a low-quality publisher who lures audiences onto their site with clickbait? They don't believe so and this author agrees!

CHAPTER NINE

FIVE GLOBAL TRUTHS, ONE BIG PICTURE

During the course of this book, we've identified and discussed in detail the Five Global Truths that make sense out of a messy media world. They are summarized as follows:

1. Global Truth #1: Convergence

Media channels that used to be separate and distinct are now coming together. Media are becoming strikingly similar, and they all involve screens!

2. Global Truth #2: Symbiosis

We are not embroiled in a battle of old vs. new media. Rather, all forms of media tend to support and reinforce each other through symbiotic relationships.

3. Global Truth #3: Circuits

Media pathways, a.k.a circuits, no longer run parallel to each other. Rather, media circuits are now open and in the hands of engaged consumers. Content can jump off one channel and onto another.

4. Global Truth #4: Brands

Media have outlived their functional utilities. No single medium has a lock on distribution pathways or the audiences it serves. Media must adopt brand management practices in order to survive and thrive.

5. Global Truth #5: Economics

Media is no longer in limited supply and high demand. We have more media than we know what to do with! Now the true value of the media lies in the content that fills the pipeline.

The Five Global Truth Form, One Big Picture

Are the Five Global Truths truly separate and distinct? Actually, they all come together to create a stunning big picture. It all starts with the idea of *convergence*. The media are coming together as opposed to growing apart. This convergence creates cooperation among channels rather than competition. When entities are similar and can benefit from each other, *symbiosis* forms. The collaboration among symbiotic systems makes it easier for content to travel off one channel and onto another. In other words, the *circuits* naturally open up.

In this open environment, no single medium can own the content or the audience. The attractors become *brands* who consistently deliver high-quality content experiences regardless of the channel. And this all fundamentally reshapes *economics*. Value shifts from the audience of any given channel to compelling content that can engage an audience on any channel imaginable. The Five Global Truths illuminate one big picture of how the media world works.

When you take a step back and think about this new media order, all of a sudden what was once chaotic starts to make a whole lot of sense. The media world doesn't look as complex. This new order that's governed by similarities and cooperation is much easier to deal with than the old one, where every single medium had to be dealt with on its own and with its own set of rules.

This coming together of media systems makes it easier

for us to remain focused on the big picture and to harness the exponential potential of media channels using the new law of energy: C^3. Really, what we're dealing with now is a new relationship between content, consumers and channels.

C (1): Content

First and foremost, we must prioritize content worth sharing. Content is the ultimate attractor in an open media system. Mediocre content, whether its primary purpose is information, entertainment or marketing, simply won't cut it. We need to focus on storytelling in ways that engage consumers across a suite of symbiotic media channels. We must develop transmedia brands that can deliver transmedia stories. This is an equal opportunity proposition: both the media and marketers can play in this space. Those who understand content-driven brand experiences will win. Whoever adapts to transmedia brand management with engaging storytelling will set the stage for integrated marketing success.

C (2): Consumers

Next, we must place consumers at the center of our efforts so that they, in turn, can accelerate brand momentum. This is much larger than "consumer insight" or "customer centricity." We must acknowledge that consumers have always been and will continue to be the most potent media channel in any media plan. We must engage consumers beyond the point of purchase to a new point of acceleration. We should think of customer lifetime value not only in terms of brand loyalty, but also in terms of brand advocacy. Engaged consumers will go to great lengths to spread a brand's marketing story. But ultimately, we must remember that consumer advocacy on our behalf is a privilege that we earn. It can't be bought.

C (3): Channels

Ultimately, we must fully embrace the exponential

potential of this new media world. It's time to let go of the old Newtonian media rules that simply don't make sense anymore. We have to understand how the media truly work together to create multi-layered and engaging consumer experiences.

Media allocations can no longer be an either/or exercise; they must now represent combinations of media that work together to round out the consumer experience. The walls between digital media and the rest of the media world must come down. The sooner we all realize that every medium imaginable is now digital, the better!

We must change what we value. A discrete audience measurement in any specific medium at any specific point in time is a very small measurement of the ultimate potential of integrated marketing communications. When consumers accelerate brand experiences across vast networks, the results are truly immeasurable. And we have to get comfortable with that! We may have explained media chaos, but it will remain a bit messy. At least now you have a five point compass to guide you along your way.

CHAPTER TEN

PUTTING NEW THINKING TO WORK

How can C³ unfold as a new media and message delivery process? For those of you who are new to the world of marketing and media, you're in great shape! You do not have to unlearn all the legacy methods that have plagued the rest of us for quite some time. And those of you who have been around for a while: go grab a clean sheet of paper. You'll need it!

You Can Implement C³ with Just a Few Simple Ingredients

Luckily, this new approach is much easier to implement than past media planning methods, which relied upon complicated media mix models and an obsession with calculating reach and frequency at the lowest possible cost. Now, we only need a few simple ingredients to get great results: We need a great, transmedia story to tell, we need engaged consumers and we need an open media architecture that empowers consumers to accelerate content across media channels and social networks. We still need to measure effects, but we can now shift the burden of measurement from optimizing opportunities to optimizing outcomes.

Start With a Good Story. Do Not Pass 'Go' Until You Have One!

For years, we have been embroiled in a heated debate. What comes first: the medium or the message? In fact, we shouldn't be starting with either of these. Rather, the first step in the process is to develop a highly engaging transmedia story. A story is much larger than a "message." A transmedia story is a brand narrative that can engage consumers across time and media channels. If we don't have the story, the rest of the process really doesn't matter.

Fund Combinations of Media That Work Together to Support the Story

Next, we need to allocate resources in a whole new way. We need to fund combinations of media that work together (in symbiosis) to reinforce key elements of the transmedia story. We can no longer fund each individual media channel in isolation; we must now fund media in combinations based upon how they work with each other. What was once separated in most marketing and media functions needs to come together.

Marketing organizations and their marketing services agencies will have to do more than coordinate efforts. They will have to truly plan and implement these efforts as one integrated experience across paid, owned and earned media. Cross-channel media planning and buying will become the norm. And as a result, there will be more marketplace incentives for the media themselves to evolve into transmedia brands that can offer marketers channel-neutral solutions.

Hand the Media Plan Over to Consumers

During the first two phases of the process, the consumer is still a recipient of content experiences controlled by the media and/or marketers. But after developing a good story and then funding the best media combinations to tell it, we have to let go and hand over control to consumers. In fact, letting consumers take the reins doesn't require much from us at all! Considering that the media circuits are wide open, we simply have to inspire and engage them to the point of acceleration.

Consumers will, by default, interact with content. They will either (a) vaporize bad content or (b) accelerate great content. Our hope is to convert consumers from message recipients to message accelerants. Think of this as a conversion phase whereby consumers become the most valuable media channel in the entire mix.

Once consumers are converted from recipients to accelerants, the media plan in the real world should no longer bear any resemblance to the media plan on paper (metaphorically, of course!) If all goes well, the scheduled movement of content across media channels will quickly go out the window. Thanks to open media circuits, great content will travel on, off and across more media touch points and reach more consumers than we can possibly imagine or measure with any degree of certainty.

Support and Reinforce an Ongoing Conversation

At this juncture, what's left for a marketer to do? Sit back and watch? Well, not exactly. A marketer's job is to continue to fuel momentum by ensuring that storytelling remains fresh, provocative, relevant and accessible. At times, marketers may need to provide additional investment in specific media clusters to reinforce specific elements of the transmedia story. A marketer's job is to listen, reflect and then respond. Marketers must now enter into partnerships with consumers and use the media as a shared resource for shaping and continuing ongoing conversations.

Measure What Truly Matters

Finally, we must measure the total outcome of our efforts. If the Five Global Truths teach us anything at all, they suggest that the media no longer work in isolation. Measuring the effects of a single media channel in an integrated media plan seems misguided when you consider the true interdependence of the media.

The traditional valuation of media audiences captures only one small slice of the total picture. We should focus less on opportunities to see a controlled marketing message and more on the collective experience and the final outcome of our efforts. We must shift our measures from the beginning of the process to the end.

And we have to accept the fact that, if all goes well, it may be impossible to measure the total reach of our efforts. Instead, we can measure what counts: return on objectives and outcomes (ROO) based upon customer sales and customer value. This is a bigger idea than tying every discrete media investment to an immediate sale. Unfortunately, many marketers are treating each media occurrence as a direct response vehicle.

Instead, we must focus on the big picture. That means worrying less about whether or not each discrete piece of the transmedia puzzle is delivering a return on investment. Here's how we'll know when we've created true value: our customers will be delighted, our brands will be healthy and our bottom line will look great to the finance types who worry about these things!

This Process Comes Straight from the Pioneers Themselves

This new process was not engineered in a conference room; rather, it was the result of observing how the pioneers (celebrated in this book) got things done. Each instance involved a powerful piece of content that capitalized on the potential of transmedia storytelling. In each situation, unique combinations of media channels worked together to engage and inspire consumers.

If the depth and breadth of media combinations described in this book is any indication of what the future holds, the possibility for collaboration among media channels appears endless! We do not have to restructure ourselves around new media pathways; rather, we need to remain flexible and open to considering how all the media can work together to tell a story.

Further, in every instance, the pioneering case relied heavily upon authentic consumer engagement. In each case, the pioneer didn't buy its way into the relationship or force a conversation. Rather, consumers opted to engage with and share the experience based upon the quality and resonance of the story. And when they truly engaged, the sky was the limit.

No one could have possibly built a media plan flowchart to predict the course of Snickers "Betty White" or Oasis *Dig Out Your Soul* until the journey was complete. But that didn't mean the pioneers remained idle. They contributed new content in additional media to keep their stories vibrant and engaging.

Finally, it's doubtful that these pioneers worried about the return-on-investment of each discrete element of the transmedia strategy that ensued. Rather, they relentlessly focused on a much bigger picture. A valuable lesson learned indeed!

CHAPTER ELEVEN

INDUSTRY REPORT CARD

How Are We Doing?

Let's reflect upon the evolution of the industry since the first edition of *Media: From Chaos to Clarity* was published. Have we seen some progress? Yes! But we haven't gone nearly far enough. In fact, in some ways we have taken a few steps backwards. We continue to cling to old beliefs and to rely too heavily on technology and Big Data to solve all of our problems. Why aren't we further along?

First and foremost, there's a big difference between "media" and the "media business." Legacy media companies can't reinvent their businesses until they figure out new ways to make money. In his book, *Misunderstanding Media*, Brian Winston outlines "The Law of Suppression of Radical Potential." It's the idea that when a new technology comes along, existing institutions will constrain its influence. This isn't a matter of avoidance; rather, it's a strategy for survival.

Remember, content—that important fuel that drives the entire media ecosystem—doesn't magically appear. The production and distribution of high quality content takes time, talent and resources. Business models need to support and sustain the content product of media companies across any and every channel. And the only way to sustain a business is to carefully manage the transition from legacy models toward new avenues for growth.

Old Habits—And Models—Die Hard

Next, marketers who can help to fund all these changes have been slow to adapt because organizational change is easier said than done. Remember, convergence is a relatively new phenomenon. Not too long ago, media were highly fragmented. And marketers, along with their agency partners, became highly fragmented as well. Marketers need to put the pieces of their organizations back together. Marketing services agencies need to rebundle themselves as well. This will take time. It might even require a whole new generation. Old habits die hard—especially when livelihoods are at stake.

Even the most integrated marketing organization will not be able to realize the potential of this new media world if they are stuck using models and tools left over from the Newtonian Era. The "factories" need to be re-tooled with machinery built for an entirely new paradigm. With advances in marketing technology and Big Data, we should be able to get there. However, if all we do is use Big Data and marketing technology to squeeze the last bits out of an old, broken process, we will still fail.

Big Data Can Help! But Only If We Use It Properly

Unfortunately, too many marketers are using Big Data to drive "small" outcomes. Recently, marketers have become obsessed with hyper targeting and direct response. Marketers are using Big Data to isolate individual consumers. Then, through marketing automation, they are chasing consumers across media destinations with ads until they click on something to make a purchase. This is far from Integrated Marketing Communications. This is not at all what the new C^3 energy formula—Content, Consumers, Channels—

requires.

Does this mean that the Five Global Truths are at odds with advances in marketing automation and Big Data? Not at all! When applied properly, marketing automation and Big Data will help us to realize new possibilities in this messy media world. What is Big Data, anyway? It's nothing more than vast numbers of discrete data points that, together, paint a behavioral picture of a consumer: a real person with a head and a heart.

It is still our job to inspire people with awesome content that engages them and compels them to accelerate our stories. Big Data doesn't change that. And what is marketing automation? It's simply a more efficient means of managing pathways. Whether the pathway is based upon customer journeys, narrative arcs or consumer behavior, we still need to build the roadmap and guide the machines to serve consumers respectfully—not to stalk them, bait them or take advantage of them in any way.

Now It's Your Turn!

You may be wondering: where can I buy the software and the fancy dashboard that allows untrained, entry-level employees to push a few buttons and optimize all this effort? Professor Don Schultz, who's credited with founding IMC at Northwestern University, chuckled as he shared the following wisdom: "The criticism that you will likely hear is: this book says nothing about how much to spend and/or how to guarantee success. It doesn't help me (the planner or whomever is developing the investment structure) in convincing the finance types that we can solve the seemingly unsolvable paid/owned/earned media riddle. What you are arguing for is a measurement of 'outcomes' rather than 'outputs.' That pushes the process into the realm of forecasting and away from accounting." As is usually the case, he's right!

The answers cannot be reduced to a one-size-fits-all equation that can be programmed into the next best-selling piece of software. If we truly believe in the power of C^3, our solutions will be as varied and unique as every great piece of content (in whatever form) and each individual consumer who is compelled to use any/all available channels to shape and share that content. We simply cannot boil this all down to a magic formula. If we could, life in the classroom and boardroom would, perhaps, be a lot easier. Not necessarily better, but easier.

This new reality will require collaboration and imagination from all sides of the industry: media, marketers and the consumers they both serve. Everyone will need to work together to shape this messy media world into an ecosystem that works for everyone.

It's time for me to head back to the classroom to inspire another generation of integrated marketers. Hopefully, this text has inspired you to think about the world of media in a whole new light! Now, it's your turn to forge new pathways in a new media world. With the Five Global Truths as your compass, you can explore an abundance of new possibilities. Perhaps, you will become the next pioneer that will continue to show us how it's done!

ACKNOWLEDGMENTS

As I wrap up the second edition of *Media: From Chaos to Clarity*, I am filled with gratitude. I am grateful for the reception that the first edition of this "little book that could" received across both industry and academia. I'm grateful for you, the reader. Your desire for a simple compass to navigate this messy media world inspired me to reevaluate the Five Global Truths, gathering new evidence along the way of how the media world is transforming before our eyes.

I am incredibly grateful to the Northwestern University Medill School of Journalism, Media, and Integrated Marketing Communications for my "Chapter Two" as a member of its esteemed faculty. Northwestern has afforded me the opportunity to collaborate with true Thought Leaders on important advancements in Integrated Marketing Communications.

While the camaraderie of amazing faculty is so gratifying, Northwestern's world-class student body also deserves my thanks. My students inspire me every day with their thirst for knowledge and their desire to transform the world. It's an honor to play a small role in their journeys.

Further, every book benefits from critical eyes and thoughtful feedback. The second edition of *Media: From Chaos to Clarity* would not have come together without the generosity of others, namely: Northwestern University Professors Don Schultz and Tom Collinger, former IMC students Justin Yeh and Teri Slavik-Tsuyuki, and Publicis Groupe's Chief Innovation Officer, Rishad Tobaccowala. You each offered insight and clarity so that this book could do its job: simply explain all the messy changes in the media world. Further, I owe many words of thanks (she'll edit them out though) to my editor, Teresa Manring. She polished the second edition manuscript to a high shine. Without her, I would be flipping verb tenses and throwing jargon your way.

Finally, I would like to thank the media, themselves. Without content and consumers and channels, I don't know what my passion would be. Perhaps I would be writing a book on baseball, instead! We'll save that story for my "Chapter Three."

REFERENCES

Chapter Two:

Ephron, E. (1997). Recency planning. *Journal of Advertising Research, 37*(4), 61-65.

Anonymous. (2008). Simon Broadbent. *Campaign,* 19.

Ephron, E. & McDonald, C. (2002). Media scheduling and carry-over effects: Is Adstock a useful TV planning tool? *Journal of Advertising Research, 42*(4), 66-70.

Krugman, H. (1972). Why three exposures may be enough. *Journal of Advertising Research,* 12(6), 11-14.

Maiville, M. (2007). *A Thin Sliced World: New Methods, Models and Systems for Media Audience Analysis.* Presented at ARF: Audience Measurement 2.0 Conference, New York, NY.

Napoli, P. (2003). *Audience Economics: Media institutions and the audience marketplace.* New York, NY: Columbia University Press.

Jenkins, H. (2006). *Convergence Culture: Where old and new media collide.* New York, NY: New York University Press.

Chapter Four:

Clifford, S. (2009, December, 15). Magazines get ready for tablets. *The New York Times,* p. B1.

Botelho, S. (2011, August, 3). All 21 Time Inc. magazines to have tablet editions by year-end. *Foli.* Retrieved from https://www.foliomag.com

Moses, L. (2011, June, 9). Hearst opens app lab. *Adweek.* Retrieved from https://www.adweek.com

Meredith Corporation. (2011, March, 15). *Meredith Corporation launches tablet editions of Better Homes and Gardens, Parents and Fitness brands on iPad.* [Press Release]. Retrieved from https://www.prnewswire.com.

Ives, N. (2011, April, 22). Conde Nast taps brakes on churning out iPad editions for all its magazines. *AdAge.* Retrieved from https://www.adage.com

Dool, G. (2016, December, 1). Conde Nast shutters print edition of Self. *Folio.* Retrieved from https://www.foliomag.com

Silva, E. (2017, November, 2). Conde Nast shutters print edition of Teen Vogue. *Folio.* Retrieved from https://www.foliomag.com

Farber, D. (2013, July, 23). CNN's Jeff Zucker trades analog dollars for digital quarters. *CNET.* Retrieved from https://www.cnet.com

Chapter Five:

Stengel, R. (2007, January, 6). A changing time. *Time.* Retrieved from http://www.time.com

Swant, M. (2016, August, 26). This study from Nielsen and Google says YouTube and linear TV help each other. *Adweek.* Retrieved from http://www.adweek.com

Nielsen. (2013, October, 7). *Nielsen launches 'Nielsen Twitter TV Ratings.'* [Press Release]. Retrieved from https://www.nielsen.com

Shearer, E. and Gottfried, J. (2017, September, 7). *News use across social media platforms.* Retrieved from https://www.journalism.org

The Association of Magazine Media. (2017). *Magazine media factbook 2017/2018.* Retrieved from https://www.magazine.org.

Pathak, S. (2012, March, 12). Behind the work: The Guardian's 'Three Little Pigs.' *Advertising Age, 83*(11).

Wolff, M. (2015). *Television is the new television: The unexpected triumph of old media in the digital age.* New York, NY: Portfolio Penguin.

Collinger, T. (2016, May, 16). *Five ways marketers can rev the consumer engagement engine.* Retrieved from https://marketingprofs.com

Chapter Six:

BBH New York. (2009, June, 29). BBH New York w*ins a Titanium Lion for 'Oasis Dig Out Your Soul'.* [Press Release]. Retrieved from http://www.prnewswire.com

Palmer, S. (2009, October, 18). *Free vs. paid: the wrong debate.* Retrieved from https://shellypalmer.com

Anonymous. (2017, September, 23). Inside the big business of being a social media influencer. *CBS News Online. Retrieved from https://cbsnews.com*

Federal Trade Commission. (2017, April, 17). *FTC staff reminds influencers and brands to clearly disclose relationship.* [Press Release] Retrieved from https://www.ftc.gov *Ftc.gov, April 19, 2017.*

Chapter Seven:

Ozanian, M. & Schwartz, P. (2007, September, 27). The World's top sports brands. *Forbes.* Retrieved from https://www.forbes.com

Badenhausen, K. (2017, May, 23). The World's most valuable brands 2017: by the numbers. *Forbes.* Retrieved from https://www.forbes.com

Interbrand (2017). *Best global brands ranking.* Retrieved from https://www.interbrand.com

Chapter Eight:

ComScore. (2007, November, 5). *For Radiohead fans, does "Free" + "Download" = "Freeload"?* [Press Release]. Retrieved from https://www.comscore.com

Van Buskirk, E. (2008, October, 16). Radiohead's In Rainbows outsold previous albums despite giveaway. *Wired.* Retrieved from https://wired.com

MediaPost. (n.d.). Revenue generated by Hulu from 2008 to 2017 (in million U.S. Dollars). *Statista - The Statistics Portal.* Retrieved from https://www.statista.com

Chapter Eleven:

Winston, B. (1986). *Misunderstanding media.* Cambridge, MA: Harvard University Press.

Printed in the USA
CPSIA information can be obtained
at www.ICGtesting.com
LVHW010338271223
767456LV00004B/313